6 YEAR

Class

Non-fiction Texts

Eileen Jones

Published in 2004 by:
Nelson Thornes Ltd
Delta Place
27 Bath Road
CHELTENHAM
GL53 7TH
United Kingdom

04 05 06 07 08 / 10 9 8 7 6 5 4 3 2 1

A catalogue record for this book is available from the British Library

ISBN 0-7487-8658-9

Illustrations by Martha Hardy, Nick Schon and GreenGate Publishing Services
Page make-up by GreenGate Publishing Services

Printed in Great Britain by Ashford Colour Press

Acknowledgements
All texts written by and copyright Eileen Jones except:

'End of the rote' by Judith Judd appeared in TES Friday magazine, March 19, 2004; 'Michael Morpurgo' from *Telling Tales: An interview with Michael Morpurgo*. Interview answers copyright © Michael Morpurgo 1999. Published by Egmont Books Limited, London and used with permission; 'Friends and locals' taken from *War Boy* published by Puffin Books, London. Copyright © Michael Foreman 1989; *The Diary of a Young Girl* by Anne Frank, edited by Otto H Frank and Mirjam Pressler, translated by Susan Massotty (Viking, 1997) copyright © The Anne Frank-Fonds, Basle, Switzerland, 1991. English translation copyright © Doubleday a division of Bantam Doubleday Dell Publishing Group, 1995. 'My life' taken from *Managing my Life* by Alex Ferguson. Reproduced by permission of Hodder and Stoughton Limited. Copyright © Alex Ferguson 1999; 'The Football Hall of Fame' taken from the International Football Hall of Fame website; 'Particular Aspects of Negligence: children' taken from *James: General Principles of the Law of Torts Second Edition* (Butterworths 1964) copyright © Lexis Nexis 2004; 'Rules of Golf' taken from *Golf Rules Illustrated Ninth Edition* copyright © The Royal and Ancient Golf Club of St Andrews and Design copyright © Octopus Publishing Group Ltd 1999; 'Hours of Work' taken from 'Child Employment for Young People' published by Croydon County Council 1999; 'Current flood situation' taken from the Environment Agency website copyright © Environment Agency 2004; 'Victoria' taken from *100 Greatest Women*: Text and illustrations © Chrysalis Children's Book Group. Reprinted by permission of Chrysalis Children's Books, a division of Chrysalis Books Group PLC; 'How does light travel' and 'How can rivers change?' reproduced from *The Usborne Internet-linked Book of Knowledge* by permission of Usborne Publishing, 83–85 Saffron Hill, London EC1N 8RT, UK. Copyright © 2003 Usborne Publishing Ltd; 'Glossary' reproduced from *The Usborne School Dictionary and Thesaurus* by permission of Usborne Publishing, 83–85 Saffron Hill, London EC1N 8RT, UK. Copyright © 2003 Usborne Publishing Ltd; 'Different types of poetry' taken from *Black's Rhyming and Spelling Dictionary* by Pie Corbett and Ruth Thomas. Reproduced by permission of A & C Black Publishers Ltd. Copyright © Pie Corbett and Ruth Thomas 2003.

Photographs: Text 5: Millennium Bridge – Alamy RF (NT); Text 39: Queen Victoria – Illustrated London News V1 (NT); Text 44: Sunlight through trees – Corel 33 (NT); Text 45: Smooth stones – Peter Adams/Digital Vision BP (NT); Text 46: Waterfall – Corel 795 (NT).

Cover image: YA016281 © Corbis/Yann Arthus-Bertrand (rights managed) Grand Prismatic Spring

Every effort has been made to trace the copyright holders but if any have been inadvertently overlooked, the publishers will be pleased to make the necessary arrangement at the first opportunity.

Contents

How to use this book

What this book contains	• Extracts from published works, plus tailor-made extracts, all arranged and chosen specifically to match the examples of medium-term planning provided by the National Literacy Strategy
	• Teaching ideas for each extract to get you started, covering some of the relevant text, sentence or word level objectives from the relevant unit
How you can use *Classworks Literacy Texts* with other resources	• The blocked unit structure means you can dip into the book to find resources perfect for what you're teaching this week – it doesn't matter what plan, scheme or other resource you're using
	• There are two *Classworks Literacy Texts* books for every year from Reception (or Primary 1) to Year 6 (or Primary 7): one contains Fiction and Poetry, the other contains Non-fiction. Both books together contain texts for every unit of the medium-term plans

What each page does

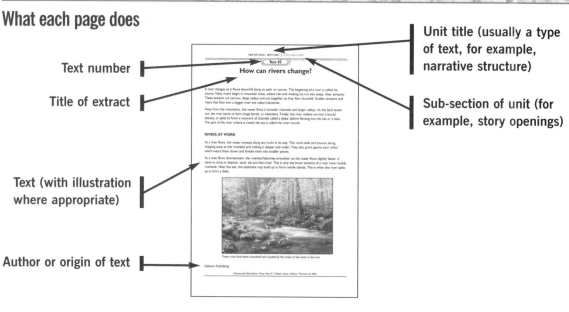

Text number

Title of extract

Text (with illustration where appropriate)

Author or origin of text

Unit title (usually a type of text, for example, narrative structure)

Sub-section of unit (for example, story openings)

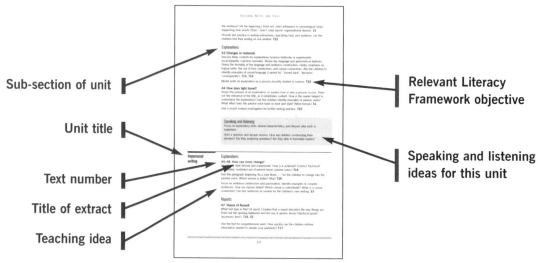

Sub-section of unit

Unit title

Text number

Title of extract

Teaching idea

Relevant Literacy Framework objective

Speaking and listening ideas for this unit

First night review

Theatre

Stunning transition from page to stage

Solomon's Wonders
Global Theatre, WC2
Box Office: 020-0832 1147

Review by Dominic Powers

Last night saw the opening at London's Global Theatre of Bec Evatt's ambitious staging of *Solomon's Wonders*. It was one year in the making; it suffered three opening night cancellations; it had a final delay of three weeks; and it was worth it all.

Whatever problems there were, not a sign of them remains. The set was literally breathtaking, as the Global's revolving stage whirled characters between present and future; lifted them into outer space, before plunging them into an underwater domain; and pitched machines against people.

Eileen Perkins's books confront difficult concepts, questioning our power to control the technology we develop, and presenting a fearsome picture of a world galloping beyond moral control. In her trilogy, it is Solomon, still young and innocent enough to display inherent restraint and caution, who can save the world. With the world hurtling towards its Armegeddon, when computers will attempt to wreak their final revenge on their makers, the fate of mankind rests with Solomon.

The two young leads playing Solomon and Esther were brave choices. Both in their first major stage productions, they bring the essential youth and energy needed in these roles. Neither lets down the director. In particular, Nik Briers is a brilliant choice. He succeeds in combining Solomon's timorous nature, with a slowly-discovered inner strength, all the time retaining his innocence and humility. Throughout the play, he remains the linchpin of the action.

Sarah Doone, as Solomon's trusted helpmate, gives convincing support, while Dan Brooke, as the cruel, vindictive teacher, gives the powerful performance we have come to expect of him.

Bec Evatt made us wait for this play. The audience will forgive her. *Solomon's Wonders* cannot be missed.

End of the rote

The idea of replacing rigid teaching styles with games-based education for primary children may be old hat here, but in Russia, the debate is just beginning.

Judith Judd reports from Moscow.

Children at Moscow's School 1674 are learning English by playing a game. "Tomorrow I will go shopping and buy a coat," says the first 10-year-old. "Tomorrow I will go shopping and buy a coat and a hat," says the next. "A coat, a hat and a scarf," continues the third. To British primary teachers the idea of learning through games may be commonplace, but in Russia the change from a timetable dominated by rote-learning and facts to one that engages children and promotes creativity is just beginning.

School 1674, a showpiece state-funded nursery and primary in spacious, gleaming quarters in the Krylatskoye suburb of the city, is one of those leading the way. Ludmilla Suprunova, the headteacher, an elegant figure in a chic black dress that wouldn't be out of place at the opera, is taking advantage of the new freedom to innovate, and is establishing the school of her dreams. In this experimental school, she says, 180 children aged between three and 10 follow "individual programmes". She says, "We do our best to make life in school interesting for our children. All our lessons are based on games. Our school is a large family and we treat our children as individuals."

But this Russian version of progressive, child-centred learning still has a more traditional look than most British nurseries and primaries. The 10-year-olds playing their English game know that today's exercise is based on the "future simple tense". Natalia Ivakova, their teacher, explains that her pupils already have a sound grasp of grammar. They know the difference between irregular and regular verbs, the present and the present continuous, adverbs and adjectives. All began learning English at the age of four, at the same time as they started to learn to read in their own language.

They sit at desks in neat rows in a large, airy classroom where the walls are mostly bare. Even in the classes for younger pupils, brightly coloured toys and dolls sit tantalisingly out of reach in glass-fronted cupboards. Questions from British journalists, invited by RIA Novosti, the Russian information agency, about sand and water play draw blank looks from the immaculately-suited teachers.

All pupils may stay at school from 7am until 6pm, and though some parents choose a shorter day, most children are there for the full 11 hours and complete their homework in school. The idea, which goes back to Soviet times, is to fit in with parents' working hours, although parents who are not working are free to leave children there if they wish.

Ms Suprunova echoes the official Russian belief that health is a vital part of young children's education: every class has a nurse and the children exercise outside for three hours every day, even in Moscow's sub-zero temperatures. Mostly they just walk, apparently uncomplainingly, but there is also skiing in winter and sledging in the playground. Porridge is served for breakfast, with plenty of vegetables and fruit juice, followed by home-baked pies for lunch.

But if the days of most Russian primary pupils are more formal and structured than those of their British counterparts, change is on the way. Vladimir Filippov, Russia's education minister at the time of The TES's visit, charged with the task of improving 63,000 schools, almost 6,000 of them with fewer than 20 students, says: "There was too much rote learning in the past, and there still is".

Times Educational Supplement

Text 3

British weather hits the headlines

How High Can We Go?

By Parvinda Bagueeri

Science Correspondent

Britain seems warmer and figures for 2003, released today by the Met Office, are the hard statistics to support human intuition.

2003

Britain

Last year was Britain's fifth warmest year ever. In the summer, the UK sweltered, with temperatures climbing steadily in July and August. The peak was set at 38.5°C on August 10 at Brogdale, near Faversham in Kent. This was not just last year's highest temperature: it was the top temperature ever recorded in Britain.

Abroad

The picture was the same elsewhere. Central Europe was uncomfortable for much of the summer, with popular tourist sites becoming almost no-go areas. France suffered particularly badly, with elderly people unable to cope with the extreme heat: France's traditional August holiday period ended with the shocking news of death from dehydration for thousands of pensioners.

Will this happen again?

This does not appear improbable. The temperatures of 2003 form only part of an ongoing, global picture. Since 1990, the world has had ten of its hottest years. Particularly striking is the fact that four of those years have been since 1997.

The Met Office is already predicting another hot year in 2004, with a 20% probability of reaching records already set.

Is the future good?

These higher temperatures are not necessarily to people's benefit. The stark reality is that people will need to adjust the way they live. In Britain, air conditioning may prove to be necessary for many people; the working day may need to exclude the hottest hours; skin protection must be improved; the threat of dehydration – particularly for the young and elderly – must be recognised as real. If the climate is changing, then the population must change with it.

It's good to talk – but it's easier to send an e-mail

Communication is about talking and listening whatever form you choose, says **Susan Pape**

WHAT IS the best form of communication in the office? Is it better to whizz off an e-mail, call a meeting, perch on someone's desk and talk face to face, or grab some gossip by the coffee machine?

According to the findings of a survey conducted by the recruitment agency Select Appointments, the majority of us communicate by e-mail. Of more than 500 people questioned, 333 said they preferred this method. Eighteen per cent – 95 people – favoured face-to-face communication, and 13 per cent – 69 people – were happier talking on the telephone. Just 1 per cent – six people – said they preferred meetings, while just three people opted for memos.

Rachel Moss, head of marketing and communications, says she was not surprised by the result. "Everyone is so used to e-mails now that it has become automatic. So much so, that when we recently had a 'No e-mails day', many people found it hard to break the habit. They had to pick up the phone or walk down the corridor to go and speak to someone."

"E-mails are especially useful when you are communicating with a group of people or when you have a large attachment to send", she says. "But they are informal and the person you are sending them to can't pick up the tone of your voice."

Moss believes that face-to-face meetings are important – whether dealing with staff or clients. "Sometimes it is better to grab someone by the coffee machine than send an e-mail and have to wait for a reply, and with clients, we always like to meet them personally first."

Maxine Brooker, a PA at Select Appointments, prefers the face-to-face approach. She sits right outside her boss's office and speaks to him regularly. "I much prefer talking to someone because then you know the question has been received and you get an answer straight away. Besides which, if you are working fairly close to someone, it seems rude to e-mail rather than to talk to them."

Brooker also receives dozens of telephone calls during the day. "Sometimes people will ring when they could have just as easily sent an e-mail," she says. "I make notes as I'm talking because my memory is so bad. But if I take a message for someone, I will write it down and deliver it in person."

Although the memo has all but gone from the office, Lynne Brennan, a writer and trainer in business etiquette, believes that memo mentality is still with us.

"We have e-mail now but there are still people who copy e-mails to the world and its wife. Communicating with someone properly if you want something done efficiently means copying e-mails only to those directly affected."

Brennan advises against using e-mail for praise or criticism. "This should only be done face-to-face," she says.

"If you are praising or criticising someone personally they can see your face and see how pleased you are, or how difficult the situation is. If you want to praise or criticise someone you are unable to see personally you can send an e-mail, but you need to think carefully about what you write before sending."

Louise Mason, a PA for American Express has been on the receiving end of harsh e-mails. "There are still people in the corporate world who think you are 'just' a PA or a secretary, and I have had e-mails that are abrupt or dismissive," she says. "Luckily, I'm thick-skinned."

Because she works with an international team based in Europe and America, she finds e-mail quick and efficient for communicating with the whole group. "But there have been times when I haven't been able to get hold of someone and resorted to text messaging on my mobile," she says. She rarely writes letters and sends faxes only to confirm hotel bookings.

"Communication systems have developed rapidly over the past few years and I think they will go on developing," she says. "But whatever happens, the important thing is to remember that communication is about talking and listening and about delivery and interpretation. If you don't explain yourself well and the person at the other end doesn't understand, then you haven't communicated at all."

The Times
Wednesday January 7th 2004

The London Chronicle

15 JUNE 2000   **SERVING THE CAPITAL**

Footbridge Falters

Movement felt on London's latest bridge

by Laura Doyle

The new Millennium Bridge had its official opening at noon on Tuesday; and by the end of the week it had been declared closed. The bridge moved. When thousands of commuters used the route between St Paul's and the Tate Modern on Tuesday evening, swaying and shaking were clearly visible.

"At first I thought it was my imagination," said the 25-year-old actress, Rebecca Bourne, currently appearing at The Globe, "but when I saw a girl lose her balance, I knew something was definitely wrong."

"Well, it was a bit of a laugh at first, but then you start to think of the real danger," echoed Chris Netwal, a 28-year-old City broker. "I will want to know what safety checks have been carried out before I go on it again."

The engineering firm responsible for the construction has indeed promised stringent checks before the bridge will be re-opened. Nevertheless, the fact remains that after problems with the London Eye and the Dome, this is another Millennium embarrassment for the Government. A trouble-free opening to this prestigious bridge was desperately needed. As it is, it has brought only intense disappointment to Londoners.

The Millennium Bridge was meant to offer pedestrians a quick and convenient link between two important and desirable areas of London; many people now wonder if that promise will ever become a working reality. It remains to be seen. The Victorians left us a legacy of bridges able to withstand the onslaught of our road traffic: we build one that fails its pedestrians within a week. Surely the London of 2000 deserves better.

Text 6

The London Chronicle

I AUGUST 2000 **SERVING THE CAPITAL**

Congestion charge looming

As traffic grinds to a halt, the Town Hall threatens charges

Report by Rupi Ohmah

Worse than usual traffic chaos in the city centre is forcing the City Council to look again at the thorny issue of congestion charges. Originally proposed in 1997, a congestion charge was then rejected, with the Council fearing that the scheme would be too unpopular with Londoners.

However, since then, an increase in car use has put further strain on London's roads.

"We can't just ignore this problem," said Jim Howlett, London's Chief Officer of Traffic. "Unless we act soon, London will reach complete gridlock."

The Council is now considering a revised version of the congestion charge scheme, with drivers charged on a daily basis, according to the zones they use. None of us will like it, but we may have to face up to it.

Heard the latest news in the playground?

Its official: skipping is bad for you!

Report by Keith Fletcher, Features Editor

This week the Head of Woodline Primary School in North London slapped a ban on skipping ropes. Her final newsletter of the school year first wished parents a happy holiday, and then gave them the bad news: their children would not be allowed to bring their ropes with them in September. The parents are incensed.

"It seems crazy," complained 32-year-old mother, Sharon Hughes.

"I've got two girls at that school, and I want to see them skipping."

"My lad belongs to a football school of excellence. He has been told that skipping will keep up his fitness. For the sake of his future, I'm going to fight this," promised Lee Smart, the father of a boy in Year 4.

It certainly seems unreasonable. Accidents can happen in any game, but in these days of obesity, we should be encouraging our youngsters to exercise, not stopping them.

Unfortunately, the Head declined our request for an interview.

Editorial	p. 7
Letters	p. 12
TV & Radio	p. 18
Weather	p. 20
Classified	p. 16
Horoscopes	p. 15

January 2003

3.00 p.m.

Weather warnings are in place for the eastern side of the country, with snow showers expec[...] next 24 hours. Drivers are advised to avoid unnecessary journeys.

5.00 p.m.

Reports are coming in of serious delays on the M11. Tailbacks have built up: 2 miles are blocked [...]een junctions 8 and 9 southbound; and the 4 miles between junctions 6 and 9 northbound are almost [...]onary. Snow showers are reducing visibility to 5 metres. Drivers are urged to avoid the motorway.

7.00 p.m.

Trips between Cambridge and London are delayed by tailbacks of 11 miles on both carriageways. Journeys between the cities are estimated to take up to 8 hours. Motoring organisations are stretched to the limit.

10.00 p.m.

The M11 has been closed in both directions. Traffic already on the motorway has been brought to a standstill. Motorists stuck in traffic jams are confronted by the possibility of lengthy delays in freezing temperatures.

11.00 p.m.

Snow is falling heavily on the eastern side of England. Snow drifts are building up on the M11, where traffic has been brought to a standstill. Stranded motorists are faced with the likelihood of a long, cold night in temperatures forecast to reach −14°.

11.30 p.m.

Fears are growing for the safety of motorists on the M11. A pregnant 29-year-old woman has been helicoptered to hospital, and it is feared that other people may have been left without their regular medication.

11.45 p.m.

The M11 is being patrolled by the Medical Motorcycle Unit. Supplies of diabetes, epilepsy and asthma drugs are being carried by the paramedics. These drugs are being distributed or administered as necessary.

12.30 a.m.

This is an important message to drivers on the M11. All motorists on the M11 should remain in their vehicles. A hot drink is being brought to all motorists, and traffic will be moving shortly. Drivers are reminded not to leave their vehicles.

1.30 a.m.

Temperatures have fallen to −16° on the eastern side of the country. Fears are growing for the safety of stranded motorists on the M11. Young and old people involved are particularly threatened by the freezing conditions. People have been instructed to stay in their vehicles. Hot soup is being taken to as many as possible.

2.00 a.m.

This is an urgent message. All occupants of cars on the M11 are to be taken to shelters for safety. Wait in your vehicle until a uniformed patrolman appears. Follow his torch and you will be led to a place of refuge. Do not move until the patrol officer collects you. Again, do not move until you are collected.

2.30 a.m.

Shelters have been set up along the route of the M11. Cars have been abandoned and motorists led to safety.

Jim Sykes, an officer with the East Rescue Force, said: "In 25 years, I've never known anything like it. None of us will forget tonight in a hurry."

Text 8

Who is Alan Gibbons?

Alan Gibbons is a very popular writer, whose books receive constant praise by children, teachers and critics. He is noted particularly for his ability to write books that appeal to boys.

He was born in Warrington, Cheshire in 1953. It was an agricultural area, and his father worked on a farm. When Alan was eight, his father had a serious accident at work: the result was that he was no longer fit for farm labouring. Consequently, he had to find factory work, and the family moved to the industrial town of Crewe.

Alan found the move unsettling, as the urban environment was very different from the village life he was used to. In interviews, he has talked about finding his new school difficult to adjust to, and being bullied by other boys.

From early on, Alan loved reading, claiming *Great Expectations*, *Treasure Island,* and *The Bobbsey Twins* among his favourites. His interest in writing grew out of his passion for reading. However, he kept very quiet about this interest, and it was some years after leaving school before his talent was to reveal itself.

After leaving school, he tried a number of different jobs, before finally settling on teaching. He was in his mid-thirties before he did his teacher training. Once he became a teacher, it seemed natural to begin writing stories for the children in his classes; it was not long before he was sending some to publishers.

His first book was published in 1990, and other work followed quickly. His main themes involved people standing up for themselves, and he perhaps used his own experiences of school life – as a pupil and a teacher – for ideas and information.

He achieved great success with *Total Football*, a series of books linked to one of his great interests: football. Other popular stories by him are *Chicken*; *Caught in the Crossfire*; and his Legendeer trilogy. In 2000, *Shadow of the Minotaur*, the first book in the trilogy, won the Blue Peter "Book I Couldn't Put Down" award.

Alan is extremely busy. He writes articles for educational magazines; gives talks to teachers and children; appears on television and radio programmes; speaks at book festivals; and yet he still manages to do his two real jobs, teaching and writing. He is now the Author in Residence at two primary schools in Merseyside, and his new books continue to appear.

Michael Morpurgo

An interview with Michael Morpurgo by Joanna Carey

Michael Morpurgo (b.1943) has written over 60 books, many short stories and even two musicals. His books have won the Whitbread Award (*The Wreck of the Zanzibar*), the Smarties Book Prize (*The Butterfly Lion*) and the Circle of Gold Award (*King of the Cloud Forests*), and several have been shortlisted for the Carnegie Medal. In addition, two novels have been adapted for television and film (*My Friend Walter* and *Why the Whales Came*).

Michael and his wife Clare were awarded an MBE in the 1999 Queen's birthday honours for services to youth, in recognition of their work for the charity *Farms for City Children*.

Michael Morpurgo and his wife Clare live in Devon, just a short distance from Nethercott Farm, one of the three "Farms for City Children" that they run. They've been married for 37 years and they have two sons, Sebastian and Horatio, a daughter Rosalind, and four granddaughters. It's a cold wintry morning when I arrive, and we sit in the kitchen. A dog called Bercelet – a handsome lurcher that I think I recognise from Michael Foreman's illustrations for Arthur, High King of Britain *– is trying to get back to sleep on the floor in front of the cooker. A huge pile of post has just arrived – letters and parcels from publishers, letters from young readers, thank-you cards from children who've been staying on the farm, invitations to literary events… and a squashy parcel from an overseas fan containing a splendid pair of hand-knitted red socks for the author. He absent-mindedly pulls them on top of those he's already wearing as he tells me about his work, and how it was he came to be a writer.*

Joanna Carey

Classworks Non-fiction Texts Year 6 © Eileen Jones, Nelson Thornes Ltd 2004

Michael Morpurgo (continued)

When did you start to write?

I began to write when I was a teacher, inspired by the wonderfully fresh, spontaneous, positive way the children reacted to the books I read to them in class. It made *me* read a lot more, and gradually I started to write my own stories.

I don't just write for children – and I suppose it's what a lot of authors say – but I write for the "child in me", "the inner child", that I suppose I still partly am. But it's rewarding to write for children – they are so much more capable of suspending their disbelief. That's not to say they lose their critical faculties, but because they themselves have such a heightened imaginative existence, they are more prepared to lose themselves in someone else's, provided of course that the story you offer them is tightly woven and convincing.

Where do the stories come from?

All over the place. Although I'm a writer of fiction, it's never a matter of pure invention. There's always a nugget of truth at the centre of each of my stories: incidents in my own life, people I've met, items remembered from TV documentaries, articles snipped out of newspapers. Anything that catches my eye, I'll hang on to it. I've got my antennae out all the time.

Certainly there's more than just a nugget of truth in one story Michael wrote recently (in The Family Tree*) – about a boy who, never having met his natural father, sees him for the first time on television.*

That episode's largely autobiographical, isn't it?

Yes. I was brought up with a stepfather and I knew almost nothing about my real father when I was a child, though I had a feeling that, like my mother, he was an actor. Television was still something of a novelty at that time – we'd bought one specially to watch Princess Margaret's wedding. And in those days there was still an air of formality surrounding the watching of a programme on television. It was an event – the curtains would be closed, people would concentrate, and there was no wandering about getting cups of coffee, no channel surfing to see what else was on. I was in my late teens, and on this occasion I was watching the Christmas film with the family – my brother, my stepbrother and sister, my mother, and my stepfather and some cousins. It was a Canadian production of *Great Expectations* and we'd just got to the terrifying scene where Pip is in the graveyard, and the escaped convict, the hideous Magwitch, looms up from behind the tombstone. My cousins were screaming with fear, then, "Oh my God!" said my mother, pointing at the screen, "That is your father!"

What had happened, as Michael was to find out later, was that when he and his brother were very small, their parents (who were indeed both actors who had met in rep at the Marlowe Theatre in Canterbury) had been separated by the war.

Joanna Carey

Friends and locals

One of my boyhood friends was aptly named "Squirt". He was small and the son of a fireman. He had a fireman's axe, the next best thing to a tomahawk. Another friend was "Wimps". Although a member of the Ship Road Gang, he was admired for eating horse dung, in the road, for a bet.

The main London Road ran along one side of the Green and was very busy, both with local traffic and the traffic of war. But the two small roads forming the other two sides of the Green were virtually unused by motor traffic, and only the occasional bike interrupted our games of street football. We played a kind of street tennis with our feet. Sometimes passing sailors or off-duty soldiers would join in and it would be several minutes before we got our ball back.

One of the small side roads trailed off into an unpaved lane full of dips and puddles known as the "Bumps". It divided Hill Green from a small dense wood and was the scene of many an ambush and highway robbery.

Our trails criss-crossed the landscape of childhood. We galloped Indian file through sage brush and tumbleweed, one hand holding an invisible rein and the other slapping the seat of our trousers.

Front doors were rarely opened, except to scrub the front step. The bike was out the back, and the back openings – the narrow lanes between the back-to-back houses – were the main thoroughfares. Nobody I knew had a car. We had no car, but we did have a piano as an ornament and a camera with no film.

Each back opening was lined with tremendously high "linen posts" carrying the clothes lines. They were as high as ships' masts. They *were* ships' masts, with ships on top. The little fleet sailed the high seas above the billowing laundry. The sheds in the back yards were where we played on rainy days. Brenda Smith and the girls were always trying to put on back-yard musicals.

A billy-goat escaped during an air raid, and we chased it into our maze of back openings. It then decided to chase *us* – in and out of back yards, biting chunks out of the hanging washing. It eventually cornered Kenny and started eating his hair. Various mums with brooms rescued Kenny and we drove the goat into the field where the fishing nets were tanned and hung out to dry. The goat was then netted as if he were a tiger. By the time the farmer arrived, his goat had eaten his way out of the net but, appetite aroused, had started on a line of drying nets.

Michael Foreman

Text 12

The Diary of a Young Girl

MONDAY, 26 JULY 1943

Dear Kitty,

Yesterday was a very tumultuous day, and we're still all wound up. Actually, you may wonder if there's ever a day that passes without some kind of excitement.

The first warning siren went off in the morning while we were at breakfast, but we paid no attention, because it only meant that the planes were crossing the coast. I had a terrible headache, so I lay down for an hour after breakfast and then went to the office at about two. At two-thirty Margot had finished her office work and was just gathering her things together when the sirens began wailing again. So she and I trooped back upstairs. None to soon, it seems, for less than five minutes later the guns were booming so loudly that we went and stood in the passage. The house shook and the bombs kept falling. I was clutching my "escape bag", more because I wanted to have something to hold on to than because I wanted to run away. I know we can't leave here, but if we had to, being seen on the streets would be just as dangerous as getting caught in an air raid. After half an hour the drone of engines faded and the house began to hum with activity again. Peter emerged from his lookout post in the front attic, Dussel remained in the front office, Mrs van D. felt safest in the private office, Mr van Daan had been watching from the loft, and those of us on the landing spread out to watch the columns of smoke rising from the harbour. Before long the smell of fire was everywhere, and outside it looked as if the city were enveloped in a thick fog.

A big fire like that is not a pleasant sight, but fortunately for us it was all over, and we went back to our various jobs. Just as we were starting dinner: another air-raid alarm. The food was good, but I lost my appetite the moment I heard the siren. Nothing happened, however, and forty-five minutes later the all-clear was sounded. After the washing up: another air-raid warning, gunfire and swarms of planes. "Oh, gosh, twice in one day," we thought, "that's twice too many." Little good that did us, because once again the bombs rained down, this time on the other side of the city. According to British reports, Schiphol Airport was bombed. The planes dived and climbed, the air was abuzz with the drone of engines. It was very scary, and the whole time I kept thinking, "Here it comes, this is it."

I can assure you that when I went to bed at nine, my legs were still shaking. At the stroke of midnight I woke up again: more planes! Dussel was undressing, but I took no notice and leapt up, wide awake, at the sound of the first shot. I stayed in Father's bed until one, in my own bed until one-thirty, and was back in Father's bed at two. But the planes kept on coming. At last they stopped firing and I was able to go back "home" again. I finally fell asleep at half past two.

Anne Frank

Classworks Non-fiction Texts Year 6 © Eileen Jones, Nelson Thornes Ltd 2004

Anne Frank
A girl who wanted to be heard

Anne Frank was born on 12th June 1929, in Frankfurt am Main in Germany. By the time she was four, Germany had become a hostile place for Jewish people. Eventually, Anne's parents made the decision to emigrate to Holland. Anne and her sister, Margot, were sent to stay with their grandmother in a different area of Germany. Three months later, Margot emigrated to Holland, and finally Anne was sent for. In February 1934 the whole family was together in Amsterdam.

Life in Amsterdam was much safer for the Frank family. However, Anne's parents worried about friends and relatives left behind in Germany, as they heard news of the increasing suffering caused by Hitler's anti-Jewish laws. Many of their relatives were persuaded to emigrate, some going to North America, and Anne's grandmother joining them in Amsterdam.

Unfortunately, Amsterdam did not remain safe for very long. Early in the war, Holland was defeated and occupied by the German Army. Harsh anti-Jewish laws were introduced there; life became more and more difficult; Anne and her family were forbidden from doing more and more; and they felt less and less safe.

For her thirteenth birthday, Anne was given a diary. So began a relationship through words. Anne treated her diary as a friend who could be told everything. The diary held the thoughts of a normal, maturing teenager; and it contained details of traumatic events. It told of the family's decision to go into hiding; secrets of their hiding place; the need to be unbearably quiet during the day; the difficulties posed by sharing the hiding place with another family; irritations caused by some of the relationships; and Anne's emotions and personal problems.

The diary was written from 12th June 1942 to 1st August 1944. Then it came to an abrupt stop: Anne's family had been found by German soldiers. The family was split up and taken to different prison camps in Poland and Germany. Anne's mother died from exhaustion and hunger; and her two daughters were killed by an outbreak of typhus early in 1945, just before the end of the war. Anne's father was the only one to survive the war.

Anne's writing was found in the family's hiding place in Amsterdam. Her father made the decision to fulfil Anne's clear wish – to have her voice heard. Consequently, Anne's diaries (they actually numbered more than one) were handed over to a publisher.

In 1947, the first publication of *The Diary of Anne Frank* was released. It was of immediate interest to people around the world, and constant reprints and translations were demanded. The family's hiding place was preserved as a museum, and continues today to draw visitors.

Classworks Non-fiction Texts Year 6 © Eileen Jones, Nelson Thornes Ltd 2004

Text 14

My life

I was born in 1819, the daughter of Edward, Duke of Kent and Victoria of Saxe-Coburg-Gotha. I too was named Victoria. My childhood was one of rigorous training, in preparation for my future role.

As a young woman, I was betrothed to Prince Albert of Saxe-Coburg-Gotha, and the wedding ceremony was conducted in 1840. I enjoyed a happy and rewarding marriage, with the blessing of nine surviving children, of whom my daughter, also named Victoria, was the eldest. She was followed by a further four girls and four boys. It was our eldest son, Edward, who became Prince of Wales and, therefore, future heir to the throne.

King William IV, my uncle, died in 1837, and I, as his rightful heir, succeeded to the throne as Queen of the United Kingdom. From the earliest days of my reign, I strove to rule wisely and morally, obeying the upbringing of my parents and the rules of my faith. Helped and supported by dear Prince Albert, the wisest and most honourable of consorts, I endeavoured to set an example to my people and to restore confidence in the wisdom and virtue of the British monarchy.

During my reign, I brought about great expansion of the British Empire. I acquired new territories, such as New Zealand in 1840, Hong Kong in 1842, Natal in 1843, and the Punjab territory of India in 1845. I sent explorers to uncharted places and, when one of my explorers, David Livingstone, discovered a site of great natural splendour, such as Victoria Falls in Africa, my name was honoured.

In war, I embraced victory, with innumerable defeats of rebellious forces in many parts of my Empire. In science and technology, I fostered change, development and progress. The Great Exhibition of 1851 – organised so wonderfully by Prince Albert – gave my people the opportunity to rejoice in their own achievements and to celebrate the progress and technical supremacy of their own country. Neither was social progress forgotten, with greater rights for my citizens, living both abroad and at home. In all, my reign brought stability to the United Kingdom.

However, last week, in the sad year of 1861, I buried my beloved Albert. I fear now that I no longer have the spirit to carry on my work alone...

Queen Victoria went on to celebrate her Golden Jubilee in 1887, before dying in 1901.

Classworks Non-fiction Texts Year 6 © Eileen Jones, Nelson Thornes Ltd 2004

Launched on the Clyde

The high standard meant that there was tough competition for team places at the major football schools, of which Govan High was one, and I was surprised soon after my arrival there to see on the noticeboard that I was to report to play trials for the Under-13 eleven. Apparently my buddy from Broomloan Road Primary, Tommy Hendry, had recommended me to the teacher in charge of the team. George Symington was his name. He looked a fearsome figure and his looks were not deceiving. Nobody trifled with Mr Symington. He achieved extraordinary success with the team and we went more than a year without losing a game.

In my first season the pinnacle was our Whitefield Cup encounter with St Gerard's, the Catholic secondary school we were always striving to beat at every age level. I don't recall any religious bitterness between the schools but the division in loyalties was always clear. Our boys supported the local heroes, Rangers, and the lads from St Gerard's were Celtic fans, which ensured that when we met there was an extra edge. The first attempt to settle our Whitefield Cup tie ended in a 1–1 draw on the big ash pitch at Pirie Park, the ground we shared with St Gerard's. It was a day of high winds and the ash gusting into the players' faces made the game a bit of a farce. We were rather fortunate to survive with a draw, although I didn't feel especially lucky when a few parents of St Gerard's players made me the target of some severe heckling. I had been attracting quite a lot of coverage in the local paper, the *Govan Press*, and the fact that I performed badly that day gave those adults an opportunity to hound me. I was taken aback by this hostility from grown men but my dad was completely unmoved afterwards and merely said that the only appropriate answer was to play well in the replay, preferably with a hat trick thrown in. That second game took place on a perfect Saturday morning. I played a blinder and did score a hat trick and we won 6–3. After striking one of my goals in at the junction of upright and crossbar from twenty yards, I could not resist celebrating in front of the St Gerard's supporters. Dad was right about the best way to shut them up.

That season we won our league, the Whitefield Cup (beating Bellahouston Academy 7–1 in the final) and the Castle Cup. In the Castle Cup our final victims, Adelphi Secondary from the Gorbals, were pulverised 6–0. We maintained our form into the following season, again capturing the league title and reaching the final of the Scottish Shield at Hampden, where we faced St Pat's of Dumbarton, who were so powerful that they had six players in the Scottish Schools team. The scoreline for that match shows that we lost 4–0 but it totally misrepresents the truth about the action. There was nothing between the two sides until our goalkeeper, Angus Birnie, broke his finger with ten minutes to go and had to go off. We went to pieces after that and lost the four goals, making it look like a slaughter. Mr Symington was devastated. He couldn't believe we had lost.

Alex Ferguson

Text 16

The Football Hall of Fame

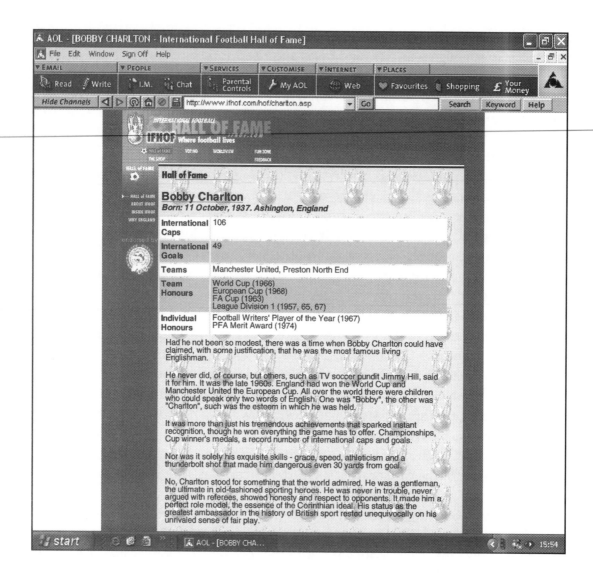

International Football Hall of Fame

Text 17

A guide to the River Severn

The River Severn flows through the heart of England. Covering a distance of 220 miles, it is acknowledged as Britain's greatest natural navigable river.

The course followed is through the counties of Shropshire, Worcestershire and Gloucestershire. The source is at Plynlimon, which is located in the Welsh mountains, and the sea is reached finally at the Bristol Channel.

The Severn can be fast-flowing, and is famed for its tidal wave. Its tide is the second highest in the world. The tidal wave, referred to as the Severn Bore, has a range of 15 metres and more with a speed averaging 10 mph.

The Severn is notorious for floods. These are suffered annually by many of the settlements located along the river. Cities and towns such as Worcester and Bewdley are threatened regularly and, in 1947, one of the river's highest floods was recorded.

The course followed by the river passes through varied scenery, with much of the countryside regarded as the most picturesque in Britain. Some stretches are recognised as particularly dangerous: the section near Gloucester has been identified as too dangerous for most users of the river. For this reason, this stretch of the river is circumnavigated by the Gloucester and Sharpness Canal, which was built during the 19th century. Downstream of Gloucester, the current remains difficult, so expert knowledge of navigation is needed.

The Severn's journey can be followed by other means of travel. The river is flanked by the Severn Way, a riverside footpath, that runs close to the river for most of its journey from Plynlimon to the Bristol Channel. The Severn Way is the longest riverside footpath in Britain.

Leisure activity is well provided for on the Severn. Upper reaches, upstream of Stourport, are used by rowers and canoeists, and tourists are taken up and down the river by cruisers. Fishing is also popular, as the Severn has remained free of the pollution problems faced by rivers such as the Thames. The Severn is fished for its plentiful supply of salmon, trout and other freshwater fish. In addition, the Severn is fished for elvers, now so rare as to be an expensive delicacy.

The animal kingdom is well catered for by the Severn. The river, particularly in its upper reaches, is used by numerous birds and insects – such as damselflies, swans and herons. It has been known for even whales and seals to travel to the river; a whale was found beached in 1885.

Classworks Non-fiction Texts Year 6 © Eileen Jones, Nelson Thornes Ltd 2004

The Thames

The River Thames is England's most famous river. Its cities and bridges are visited by tourists from across the globe.

Physical details

The course of today's Thames is about 20,000 years old. The river is carried 350km, from its source in the Cotswold Hills, through London, to its estuary into the North Sea. On its journey, the river is fed by numerous tributaries.

River characteristics

During its meanderings, the nature of the river is changed continually: a slow, peaceful river at Radcot, it has turned into a tidal river by the time it is downstream of Teddington Lock.

River settlements

Large settlements have grown up alongside the Thames, many of them famous for their universities, beautiful buildings and ancient links with the past. The cities of Reading, Oxford and, of course, London, have all grown up alongside the Thames. Other settlements that have developed beside the Thames have adopted the river's name: Henley-on-Thames and Kingston-upon-Thames are river towns close to London.

River buildings

Many of the bridges built to cross the Thames are famous in their own right. London's Tower Bridge presents an imposing neighbour to the Tower of London and the dreaded Traitor's Gate. The new Millennium Bridge, which was built to mark the second millennium, is nicknamed "the wobbly bridge", because of the movement felt as too many people used the footbridge when it was first opened.

Uses

The Thames is a working tourist attraction: it is used as a means of transport, a leisurely alternative to rail and road. Its cruisers can be seen daily, transporting visitors between famous landmarks – such as Westminster, the Tower of London and Hampton Court Palace.

River threats

London is well protected from dangers posed by its river. The Thames Barrier, which was built in 1982, is a solid protection of moving steel gates, designed to protect the city from floods. Nevertheless, the figures recorded have shown a gradual rise in the river's tides, with the blame for this placed on global warming. There may come a time in the 21st century when the height of the barrier will need to be raised.

Animal habitats

In recent times, strong measures have been taken to improve the cleanliness of the river. Consequently, the Thames has become a safe breeding area for many animals. Many species of fish, which had previously abandoned the polluted Thames, are found in this river again.

Flooding

The rain continues to fall heavily, and reports are coming in of hazardous driving conditions in the south of the region. An increasing number of roads are becoming impassable, and severe weather warnings are now in place for South Birmingham, Warwickshire and North Oxfordshire.

Part of the A46 is now closed to traffic. With large sections of it already under water, the road has been closed between Evesham and the Warwick University junction, south of Coventry. Routes south of Stratford-upon-Avon are being affected by flash floods, so there are real fears that the town may find itself totally cut off. The evening rush hour begins in an hour's time; the situation then is impossible to forecast. The police and motoring organisations are working together to highlight danger spots, but there are concerns about the problems that the rush hour will bring. Motorists are strongly urged to check on current information before setting out on any journeys, and to have a torch, food and drink, a blanket, and warm clothing in the car with them.

Farmers need to start moving animals onto higher land. Regular advice is available on the Farmer's Channel, 62.5 medium wave. In the Priors Hardwick area, where sheep are marooned, supplies and assistance are being airlifted in.

As yet, the M40 motorway remains open but with use restricted to a single carriageway. The police are appealing to drivers to avoid the motorway. Heavy spray has reduced visibility to 25m, making driving conditions very dangerous.

No trains are running between Leamington and Banbury, as the track is under water. The commuters who travel into Leamington daily, are likely to be trapped there overnight. In the town itself, the River Leam is perilously swollen, but the situation is being monitored closely. Householders living close to the Trinity Bridge will receive deliveries of sand bags during the next few hours. Everyone can feel confident that the emergency services are equipping all homes in the danger zone.

Homes should be sand-bagged by residents as soon as possible. Householders are advised to keep a radio on, and to be ready to evacuate their homes. People are requested to be alert to the welfare of elderly neighbours.

There is no sign of a let up in the rain, but the public should be confident that the emergency services are ready to take any action needed. Weather and travel news will be broadcast on this channel every 20 minutes. Stay tuned in.

Classworks Non-fiction Texts Year 6 © Eileen Jones, Nelson Thornes Ltd 2004

Report on flood damage to local area

The damage inflicted by the recent flooding is considerable, but is being dealt with. Extra money is required for renovation and repair of properties and an application has been made for an extraordinary payment from the Government. An answer is expected within the next few weeks but there is no reason to believe that the application will not be treated favourably. This report sets out the areas that have given most concern.

Dwellings

Dwelling places are being given priority. All available county housing funds are being directed to this area. An emergency payment of £500 is given to any person who has suffered ground floor flooding; and a payment of £1000 is given to persons who have suffered flooding to higher storeys. Where required, temporary accommodation is made available for families with young children and to people over the age of 75. All other cases are judged according to need.

Structural repairs

Private arrangements are made by home owners with private insurance. People are warned against committing themselves to repair bills before insurance payments have been confirmed.

Council tenants are dealt with according to the Needs Register: that is, families with young children, and people over 75 being attended to first. All council tenants have now been seen for an initial assessment and no tenant is being left in a dangerous environment.

Furnishings

Assistance with the cost of the cleaning or replacement of damaged furnishings is made by the County Council in the emergency payments of £500 and £1000. Many people are further reimbursed by their own insurance. Government money may mean that an additional payment may be offered to all those in real need, but such a payment will not be made until after the extraordinary payment, if granted, is received from the Government.

In the case of hardship, application for further help may be made at the County Council Hardship Department, Squadron Place, Lemwick.

Local Authority schools

The primary schools in Lightheath and Little Dene have been closed. Flood damage inflicted on classrooms and computer rooms has made the schools unusable. Repairs are being completed as quickly as possible. In the meantime, vacant school places at Wilford and Cotton Dene are being used, with children from the other two villages being bussed there daily. It is hoped that this temporary measure can be brought to an end in the coming month.

Business properties

Many small businesses are closed. This state of affairs is likely to remain until insurance claims have been dealt with.

Many small communities are suffering badly, because of the closure of village shops. It is hoped that Government financial help can be allocated to many of these essential retailers.

When the severity and extent of the flooding is considered, great fortitude and resilience has been displayed by local people.

Classworks Non-fiction Texts Year 6 © Eileen Jones, Nelson Thornes Ltd 2004

Text 21

Food for the Ancient Greeks

The diet followed by the people of Ancient Greece was a healthy one. This was thanks to its strong reliance on natural resources, readily available in Greece.

Fruits

Fruit was an important element of the Greek diet. The growth of fruits such as figs, melons, dates, pomegranates, grapes and olives was encouraged to flourish by the hot, sunny Mediterranean climate. Wine was produced using the grapes. Similarly, additional uses were found for olives, as the oil yielded by them fulfilled a number of needs:

- olive oil has known health-giving properties;
- it is an important cooking ingredient;
- it can be used as a fuel;
- it can be used as a liquid for cleaning.

Vegetables

The vegetables grown and eaten included onions, beans, peas and turnips. In addition, garlic was a prized vegetable and was used unsparingly. The liberal use made of this vegetable was wise: it is known today that garlic not only flavours food, but it also helps the human body ward off many infections.

Cereals

The main cereals farmed were barley and wheat.

Flesh

A considerable amount of fish and seafood was eaten by the people of Ancient Greece, but only if they lived near the sea. As for meat, reliance was placed on animals kept on people's farms: sheep, goats, or pigs. Nevertheless, only a small amount of meat was consumed by the poor; meat eating was regarded as a luxury, which was available to the rich.

Meals

The main meal of the day was taken in the evening, with breakfast and lunch kept small. Large, indulgent dinner parties were sometimes enjoyed by the rich: numerous courses were served, accompanied by a liberal amount of wine. However, only men were allowed to be present at these occasions.

Text 22

The modern use of the ideas of Ancient Greece

The modern world still has numerous links with Ancient Greece. The origins of many modern traditions, the ways of living, speaking and behaving, can be traced to that civilization.

Language

Most of today's European languages contain some vocabulary which is rooted in a Greek word. In particular, many words linked to the fields of medicine, science and the arts may be found to have their origins in the language of the Ancient Greeks. *Drama*, *theatre*, *philosophy*, *astronomy*, *psychology*, *neurology* and *haematology* are just some of the English words to which that rule applies.

Knowledge

Some of the world's greatest thinkers were Ancient Greeks. The discoveries made by those philosophers have been passed down to the modern world. The names, beliefs and teachings of men such as Aristotle and Socrates are still revered today. Hippocrates, who founded modern, scientific medicine, is honoured in the Hippocratic Oath, sworn by every new doctor; and Plato's wise philosophical writings are still studied as academic texts.

Government

The Ancient Greek ideal was based on fairness. The Greeks' concept of states, in which government was run by councils made up of citizens, is mirrored in 21st century *democracies*; this was the name given to the political system of Ancient Greece, in which ordinary citizens were enfranchised, giving them a part to play in decision-making. It is a name that 21st century societies have not changed.

Sport

Today's global celebration of physical prowess, the Olympic Games, held every four years, has its roots in the Olympic Games of Ancient Greece. They too, were held every four years, in honour of Zeus, the king of the gods, all of whom lived on Mount Olympus. Each modern celebration of the Olympic Games is a reminder of that link with the past.

Physical remains

Written records of the history, beliefs, lives and stories of the Ancient Greeks are still to be found in the world's literature and museums. The ancient splendour and beauty of the Parthenon, Athens's majestic temple, continues to be wondered at; and modern architects are still inspired by its classical form. Carved stone, and pieces of painted pottery have been unearthed by archaeologists, providing priceless museum artefacts. Many of the treasures of the 21st century originate from the Ancient Greeks.

Text 23

Dear Mr Whallen

Flat 5
Nelson House
Trafalgar Estate
Keneaton
KV2 XR8

4th February 2004

Mr A Whallen
Trafalgar Estate Council Representative
Councils Offices
Northgate
Keneaton

Dear Mr Whallen

I have a proposal that I would like you to put forward at the next meeting of the Town Council. The proposal is for the permanent return of the skateboarding ramp in Talisman Square.

I am a thirteen-year-old, and I can assure you that there is not much to do in this town! School holidays can be particularly boring times, with August often the worst of the lot. Last year was brilliant, because we all had something to do. Some of us were on the ramp all day; this meant that stupid people, who often get themselves into trouble for throwing litter around, were kept busy for once. I would have thought that pleased everyone.

I know that a lot of our parents are willing to help with the work of getting it all ready – therefore, it would not cost very much, or take too long. As for the people who live nearby, well, I was surprised last year by how many of them seemed to enjoy sitting on the benches in the Square and watching us. I suppose that, as many of them live alone, they enjoy the entertainment and company.

I hope you will be able to persuade the Town Council to agree to this proposal.

Yours sincerely

Matt Doyle

Matthew Doyle

Dear Ms Clarke

14 Waverley House
Keneaton Gardens
Keneaton
KV1 FL6

4th March 2004

Councillor J Clarke
Council Offices
Northgate
Keneaton

Dear Ms Clarke,

I am writing to you with some concern, having heard rumours of the permanent installation of a skateboarding ramp in Talisman Square. I beg you to speak out vehemently against any such proposal at the next meeting of the Town Council.

I remember your stand last year, when you were the only Councillor to voice concern about noise pollution in the town, so I know that you will be sympathetic to my concerns about excessive noise from this equipment. Constant bangs prevented me getting to sleep last August, with the result that my doctor had to increase my medication. I am sure that everyone thinks that a person's health is more important than playing on skateboards.

Of course, I am aware that young people need places to play, but Keneaton already has a very suitable park, with lovely facilities that my children used when they were young. In addition, the park, because it is surrounded by family properties, is a far more appropriate gathering place for children than Talisman Square. After all, most of us in this area are elderly.

I hope that I, along with fellow residents of Waverley House, may rely on your help. The worry about all this is not doing any of us any good.

Yours sincerely,

Rachel Bowyers.

Rachel Bowyers (Mrs)

Proposed building of a skateboarding ramp in Talisman Square (For)

Keneaton Town Council is holding its monthly meeting. Sandy Whallen has a proposal to put forward...

There is a disused site in the middle of town and it is ideal for teenagers. Talisman Square should be used as the site for a skateboarding ramp. Arguments in favour of this are numerous.

First there is an urgent need for facilities for the youngsters in this town. Apart from school sport, there is no outlet for their energy. Inevitably, boredom is forcing many of them into mischief. Have you forgotten last year already? There was the New Year fiasco with the public fountain; the mindless graffiti in the two nearby telephone kiosks; there were the broken windows in Abbey End. Need I go on?

Acts like these are not usually malicious, but they are regrettable and unpleasant. They result from a surplus of energy: harnessing that energy would make life immeasurably more pleasant for us all. A skateboarding ramp can solve our problems. After all, we already have the proof:

- In August 2003, free skateboarding was made available in Talisman Square.
- In August 2003, the number of anti-social incidents fell by 50%.

The experiment speaks for itself.

Of course, there is the cost. However, that can be kept very low. If we can all work together, volunteer our services for digging foundations, putting the supports in place, mixing and pouring concrete, then the savings will be astounding. As a result, a valuable, prized facility will be almost free. So the town itself will prosper. How many of us want to live in a ghost town – a town where house prices fall because no one wants to live here? If we want to remain a thriving community, then we need to move with the times, otherwise Keneaton will collapse, becoming a town that families reject. Think what happens then:

- school rolls fall;
- shops close down;
- local businesses struggle;
- public transport is removed.

If anyone is sceptical about this alarming picture, then they have only to think about Reek Wootton's fate in the last two years. Yes, it is a sobering picture, isn't it? Reek Wootton is a warning to us all of what happens when people do not find what they need in a town. What has happened to most of the shops? Does it still have a post office? Do Reek Wootton children enjoy being bussed to a school eight miles away? We all know the answers, and we do not want the same to happen here.

So what do we do next? We move with the times. We recognise that young people matter. We start work on a skateboarding ramp now.

Classworks Non-fiction Texts Year 6 © Eileen Jones, Nelson Thornes Ltd 2004

Proposed building of a skateboarding ramp in Talisman Square (Against)

Councillor Jane Clarke has an opposing view…

Keneaton is an historic market town: a modern skateboarding ramp is contrary to its whole image. It must not blight the town centre.

Keneaton plays host to thousands of tourists every year. Do they hope to see a skateboarding ramp? Of course not. They come to see our castle, our traditional buildings, and our quaint tea rooms: they do not come to see modern gimmicks that are available anywhere. Once we change the special atmosphere of this town, the tourists will stop coming.

If that happens, then what happens to us? You know only too well that the majority of us depend on tourists for our income. If they go, then we should pack up as well. There will be no chance of prosperity in Keneaton.

There is another important point: safety. In order to comply with new, strict regulations, regular inspections of a skateboarding ramp are mandatory; in addition, there has to be a trained supervisor in attendance. Just who will pay for that training, as well as footing the salary cost? You and I can think of better uses of our taxes.

Even then, will there be accidents? The question is not worth asking. Mix teenagers and dangerous equipment, and the consequence will be an accident. Of course, adventure is healthy, but a responsible Town Council does not have to authorise reckless danger in this way. Consider these facts:

- In August 2003, free skateboarding was made available in Talisman Square.
- In August 2003, the number of visits to A & E increased by 50%.

The figures speak for themselves, don't they?

Then there is the noise. Admittedly, Talisman Square is a free, open space, but it is enclosed by residential buildings, many of which are flats occupied by elderly townspeople. Do they want to stay awake into the early hours? Do they enjoy listening to the constant thump of a ramp in use? Talisman Square is their closest open area, so surely their needs must take precedence. We are wrong to invade their privacy.

So what can we do for our teenagers? We can improve what we already have: the park facilities. We can add a tennis court and a football pitch. Above all else, we can set an example: the town and other residents deserve respect.

Text 27

The Chairman's report

KENEATON TOWN COUNCIL
A PLACE FOR ALL

CHAIRMAN'S REPORT

SUBJECT: Proposed siting of skateboarding ramp in Talisman Square

DATE: 24 March 2004

A proposal has been put forward for the placing of a skateboarding ramp in Talisman Square. Arguments for and against the said scheme have been heard.

In favour of this introduction, Talisman Square is a vacant, central point. If a ramp were placed there, it would provide a facility for young people from all areas of the town. A skateboarding ramp has already proved a popular facility, as shown by the trial of August 2003. The trial brought a concurrent reduction in vandalism: this would be a likely future benefit, so cutting Council repair costs.

A further benefit could be in sustaining the viability of the town, as such a facility would be likely to encourage young families to live here.

Against the venture, there is cost. Voluntary help may be available, but professional expertise would be essential. Unless all Health and Safety requirements were complied with, the ramp could not be used; therefore, the cost of site inspection and staff training and employment would have to be budgeted for. Some accidents would still be likely.

Moreover, if tourists were to find the ramp an obtrusive eyesore, the town's tourism industry, its main support, could suffer. The ramp could also prove intrusive for elderly people in that area.

In conclusion, it is the opinion of the Chairman that the venture should go ahead, but with certain stipulations:

- The site should be moved to the park, an area surrounded by family housing, which is separate from both the tourist attractions of the town centre and accommodation for the elderly.

- The cost should be met by savings made by the reduction in vandalism repairs, with a further contribution from the town's lottery grant.

This decision should be reviewed after six months.

A Wood

Arthur Wood

Town Council Chairman

Proposition for debate (For)

"This class believes that the school year should be divided into four terms."

*The **Proposer** has his speech ready for the Year 6 debate...*

Madam Chair

I propose that the school year be divided into four terms. I intend to offer many strong reasons for supporting this move.

In the first place, four terms would provide balance. The structure would allow schools to divide the year into terms of similar length, consequently making planning for the teaching of the National Curriculum far simpler.

Secondly, four terms would suit the 21st century. The present division of the school year is out-of-date, as it is based on a time when most children were needed at home for an extended period, to help with harvesting. In our modern society, this is no longer the case. As a result, the long summer holiday could and should be dispensed with. This would afford great benefits to all:

- pupils would find it easier to move on from term to term, because they would not have had time to regress academically;
- teachers would find it easier to take on a new class, because the children would not have had time to forget previous learning;
- if holidays were not absurdly long, parents would have fewer problems with childcare arrangements;
- if holidays were shorter, children would not become bored.

In addition, think of the higher standards that would be achieved. The shorter summer holiday would result in improved academic results at every stage. There would be particular benefits to children making the transition from Key Stage 2 to Key Stage 3, which research highlights as an area of concern: the reduced time lapse between schools would mean that children started secondary school feeling more confident and relaxed. As a result, they would be more successful.

Furthermore, there is the health of the teacher to consider. Many teachers find a long term a strain on their mental and physical health; shorter terms, with regular breaks, would result in far less sickness. As a consequence, there would be less absenteeism: if teachers were not absent, then no expensive supply cover would be needed. The result would be that the school would have surplus money to spend on beneficial resources, such as additional sporting facilities.

The final point in my argument must rest with the pupil. School is for the pupil, and the pupil's education. Unless the best use is being made of people, time and energy, that education will suffer. Pupils require their teachers to be energetic and confident, if they are to have the best chance of achieving success.

For these reasons, I propose that the school year should be divided into four terms.

Classworks Non-fiction Texts Year 6 © Eileen Jones, Nelson Thornes Ltd 2004

Text 29

Proposition for debate (Against)

"This class believes that the school year should be divided into four terms."

*The **Opposer** has her speech ready for the Year 6 debate…*

Madam Chair

I oppose this proposition. I believe it would be wrong to divide the school year into four terms. I intend to present many strong reasons for this opinion.

First, a long summer holiday is part of British tradition. If the school year were split into four terms, this long break would not be possible and an historical system would be destroyed. The present system works well, so there is no reason for change.

Secondly, a long break from school gives families time together. Unless they have this time, their relationships may suffer, thereby increasing the number of family breakdowns. If the long break stays in July and August, then numerous, important benefits remain:

- many industries have their holiday weeks during this period, so the whole family has the chance to be together;
- British holiday resorts plan to have their facilities open at this time - unless they have the long school holiday to count on, they may go out of business;
- British weather is at its best, so healthy outdoor activities can be enjoyed;
- unless people have an adequate amount of sunshine, their bodies suffer a deficiency of Vitamin D.

Furthermore, there is the well-being of teachers to consider. Many of them are both teachers and parents. The long summer holiday is an important part of their lives, allowing them to combine both roles happily, because they can devote an extended period of time to their own children. If the long break were abolished, many of those teachers might leave the profession. As a consequence, Britain's present shortage of teachers would worsen.

In addition, think about academic standards. A shorter summer holiday could result in tired children, still exhausted from their efforts in the previous class, being unable to cope with the difficulties of a higher class. This would be a particular danger for children making the transition from Key Stage 2 to Key Stage 3. Research shows that children worry about this move: if we do not supply a good break between the two stages, then the problem could worsen. As a result, the pupils would make a less successful start to Key Stage 3.

The final point in my argument lies with the child. The school year is not just about education at school, it is also about life at home. Unless the right balance is achieved between school and home, that education may suffer. Only if pupils and teachers are happy, will pupils achieve academic success.

For these reasons, I oppose the proposition that the school year should be divided into four terms.

Classworks Non-fiction Texts Year 6 © Eileen Jones, Nelson Thornes Ltd 2004

The Chair's summing up of the debate

*The **Chair** summarises the points made by the different sides…*

The proposition before the class is as follows:

"This class believes that the school year should be divided into four terms."

Arguments in favour of the proposition are as follows:

1. Balance would result from terms of equal length, making curriculum planning and teaching easier.
2. As the long summer holiday was timed for harvesting, it no longer has relevance.
3. A shorter time lapse between ending and starting school years would obviate against holiday boredom, relieve child-minding problems and raise academic standards.
4. The absence of long terms would improve the health and energy of pupils and teachers.
5. Resulting savings from reduced staff absences would allow for the purchase of extra facilities.

Arguments opposing the proposition are as follows:

1. The long summer holiday is an essential part of the British tradition.
2. British resorts depend on July and August revenue.
3. The long break offers an opportunity to be outside, in sunshine, gaining vital Vitamin D.
4. Parent teachers want that time with their own children, if they are to stay in the profession.
5. Exhaustion could result from the loss of the extended holiday, thereby lowering academic standards.

There are strengths and weaknesses in the points made by both sides. It is true that we no longer have to adhere to a farming calendar, but change for its own sake is not essential. However, the length of the holiday does present many parents with problems over childcare arrangements.

At present, staff absences are not generally high, so changing the school year may not be of benefit. Vitamin D is indeed essential for health, but the school day offers enough outdoor time for average needs. As for academic standards, further research would be needed before it could be shown that the length of the summer holiday has any direct bearing on educational results.

Particular aspects of negligence: children

(v) CHILDREN

The fact that a visitor happens to be a child is one of the factors that the Act exemplifies as relevant for determining the standard of the "common duty of care". It provides that

"An occupier must be prepared for children to be less careful than adults" (*j*).

This provision can only be understood in the light of the pre-existing law. It was well established by numerous decisions that occupiers must be especially careful in their dealings with visiting *children*. In particular, it has long been recognised that some things, such as poisonous berries (*k*), trains (*l*), turntables (*m*), railways generally, and vehicles (*n*), are "allurements" to children in the sense that they both attract them and at the same time possess inherent dangers which they will not usually appreciate (*o*). The tale of the Pied Piper, like all good tales, is not without its counterparts in reality. The occupier must therefore be on his guard against the danger of such things to youthful visitors; and if he fails in this respect he will be liable to a child in circumstances in which he would not usually be liable to an adult who chose to meddle with things upon his property. This may be illustrated by *Glasgow Corporation v. Taylor* (*p*). A boy aged seven picked and ate some attractive-looking berries growing on a shrub in a public park controlled by the appellants; these berries being poisonous, the boy died. Although the appellants were aware of the poisonous nature of the berries (*q*) and also knew that children frequented the part of the park where the shrub was, they had done nothing to fence it off or give effective warning intelligible to children of its inherent dangers. The appellants were accordingly held liable in an action by the father of the deceased child.

What does or does not constitute an allurement or a trap to children is essentially a question of fact (*r*), and so is the question whether the occupier has taken reasonable steps to prevent injury to the child in all the circumstances.

Child visitors also often give rise to a further difficulty. It has been seen that the occupier's acquiescence in the presence of trespassers may, in proper cases, promote the trespasser to the status of a visitor, and consequently the burden of the occupier's obligation to such entrants is increased. This applies with particular force in the case of child-entrants.

(*j*) Occupiers' Liability Act, 1957, s. 2 (3) (a) (37 Halsbury's Statutes (2nd Edn.) 834). And see *Reffell v. Surrey County Council*, [1964] 1 All E. R. 743.

(*k*) *Glasgow Corporation v. Taylor*, [1922] 1 A. C. 44.

(*l*) *Gough v. National Coal Board*, [1953] 2 All E. R. 1283; [1954] 1 Q. B. 191.

(*m*) *Cooke v. Midland Great Western Rail Co. of Ireland*, [1909] A. C. 229.

(*n*) *Creed v. John McGeogh & Sons, Ltd.*, [1955] 3 All E. R. 123.

(*o*) Some things, without necessarily being "allurements", may also be hidden dangers or "traps" to children though not to adults: *Williams v. Cardiff Corporation*, [1950] 1 All E. R. 250; [1950] 1 K. B. 514 (bank with broken glass).

(*p*) [1922] 1 A. C. 44.

(*q*) Before the Act it was probably essential to liability that the inherent dangers of the attractive object should be known to the occupier, or at least be dangers of which he ought to know (see *Sutton v. Bootle Corporation*, [1947] 1 All E. R. 92, 97; [1947] 1 K. B. 359, 369). This is presumably still the case.

(*r*) Although it is one for the *court* to determine: *Latham v. R. Johnson & Nephew, Ltd.*, [1913] 1 K. B. 398, 416; per HAMILTON, L.J.

James: General Principles of the Law on Torts second edition

Rules of golf

6–4. Caddie

The player may have only one *caddie* at any one time, under penalty of disqualification.
For any breach of a *Rule* by his caddie, the player incurs the applicable penalty.

6–5. Ball

The responsibility for playing the proper ball rests with the player. Each player should put an identification mark on his ball.

6–6. Scoring in Stroke Play

a. Recording Scores

After each hole the *marker* should check the score with the competitor and record it. On completion of the round the marker shall sign the card and hand it to the competitor.

b. Signing and Returning Card

After completion of the round, the competitor should check his score for each hole and settle any doubtful points with the *Committee*. He shall ensure that the *marker* has signed the card, countersign the card himself and return it to the Committee as soon as possible.

PENALTY FOR BREACH OF RULE 6–6b:
Disqualification.

c. Alteration of Card

No alteration may be made on a card after the competitor has returned it to the *Committee*.

d. Wrong Score for Hole

The competitor is responsible for the correctness of the score recorded for each hole on his card. If he returns a score for any hole lower than actually taken, he shall be disqualified. If he returns a score for any hole higher than actually taken, the score as returned shall stand.

Note 1: The *Committee* is responsible for the addition of scores and application of the handicap recorded on the card – see Rule 33–5.

Note 2: In four-ball stroke play, see also Rule 31–4 and –7a.

6–7. Undue Delay; Slow Play

The player shall play without undue delay and in accordance with any pace of play guidelines which may be laid down by the *Committee*. Between completion of a hole and playing from the next *teeing ground*, the player shall not unduly delay play.

PENALTY FOR BREACH OF RULE 6–7:
Match play – Loss of hole; Stroke play – Two strokes.
Bogey and par competitions – See Note 2 to Rule 32–1a.
Stableford competitions – See Note 2 to Rule 32–1b.
For subsequent offence – Disqualification.

Note 1: If the player unduly delays play between holes, he is delaying the play of the next hole and, except for bogey, par and Stableford competitions (see Rule 32), the penalty applies to that hole.

Note 2: For the purpose of preventing slow play, the *Committee* may, in the conditions of a competition (Rule 33–1), lay down pace of play guidelines including maximum periods of time allowed to complete a stipulated round, a hole or a stroke.

In stroke play only, the Committee may, in such a condition, modify the penalty for a breach of this Rule as follows:

First offence – One stroke;
Second offence – Two strokes;
For subsequent offence – Disqualification.

The Royal and Ancient Golf Club of St. Andrews

Classworks Non-fiction Texts Year 6 © Eileen Jones, Nelson Thornes Ltd 2004

Text 33

Ill-health retirement

In the normal course of events, a pension may not be claimed until the employee passes the age of 60. However, in the case of ill-health which necessitates retirement from your pensionable employment below the age of 60, you can apply for ill-health benefits. In order to qualify for the said benefits, you must have completed one of the qualifying periods (refer to page 8).

Restrictions

Ill-health benefits cannot be awarded to a company employee who has been barred for malpractice, or who is under investigation by the Company Trust with a view to barring, or who is in receipt of pension benefits under the permanent retirement scheme. In a case where an employee under investigation is not then barred, payment of benefits and appropriate interest will be backdated.

Payments

Ill-health benefits are usually made up of a single lump sum and an annual pension. Calculations follow the explanation given for retirement benefits, as set out on pages 8 and 9.

Normally, ill-health benefits cannot be received by someone who is already in receipt of pension benefits under the permanent retirement scheme. Certain circumstances may warrant deviation from this condition (refer to page 10).

Employment qualifications

There are, however, particular conditions if you have resumed pensionable employment with the Company on or after 31 March 2003 and have opted back into the Company Pension Scheme, and then suffered a physical relapse. In such a case, you may be able to apply for ill-health benefits, but it would be necessary to satisfy the Company Medical Officer that you had become unfit for employment during the time of the subsequent period of pensionable employment.

In most cases, when ill-health begins during the employee's pensionable period of employment, the Company makes financial compensation for the working period lost. Qualification for such financial compensation is gained if you have had 4 years or more full-time employment in the Company's service, or 7 years part-time employment. In either case, application for such financial compensation must be made to the Company Trust within 4 months of leaving the Company's service.

Extraordinary ill-health benefit

In respect of an employee whose service falls short of the qualifying period of pensionable employment, an extraordinary ill-health benefit may be paid according to the length of service by the employee (refer to page 11).

Hours of work

CROYDON COUNCIL
Education

CHILD EMPLOYMENT

FOR

YOUNG PEOPLE

Are you thinking of getting a part-time job?

Have you already got a part-time job?

Then you need an Employment Permit.

The information in this leaflet is for general guidance only.

If you would like more information please contact
Education Welfare Service on
020 8684 4969

Other leaflets available on child employment:

Employers
Parents or Guardians

HOURS OF WORK

AGES 13 & 14

TERM TIME

Maximum of 12 hours a week.
Maximum of 2 hours on any school day between 7–8 a.m. and 5–7 p.m.

SATURDAYS & SCHOOL HOLIDAYS

Maximum of 25 hours a week when not required to attend school.
Between 7 a.m. and 7 p.m. a maximum of 5 hours a day.

SUNDAYS

Between 7 a.m. and 7 p.m. a maximum of 2 hours.

AGES 15 & 16

TERM TIME

Maximum of 12 hours a week.
Maximum of 2 hours on any school day between 7–8 a.m. and 5–7 p.m.

SATURDAYS & SCHOOL HOLIDAYS

Maximum of 35 hours a week when not required to attend school.
Between 7 a.m. and 7 p.m. a maximum of 8 hours a day.

SUNDAYS

Between 7 a.m. and 7 p.m. a maximum of 2 hours.

REST BREAKS

A child may not work for more than 4 hours without a rest break of 1 hour.

SCHOOL HOLIDAY EMPLOYMENT

There must be at least two consecutive weeks without employment during school holidays.

Croydon County Council, based on the leaflet dated November 1999

Hours of work (continued)

CHILD EMPLOYMENT

Children & Young Persons Act 1933 to 1963
Education Acts 1944 to 1996
Children Act 1989
Children (Protection at Work) Regulations 1998
Croydon Council Byelaws 1998

Child employment also falls within a large variety of other Acts and Regulations including Health and Safety (Young Person's) Regulations 1997.

You are employed if you work for a company which makes a profit whether or not you receive pay or reward for the job you do.

REGULATIONS OF EMPLOYMENT

- You are not allowed to work under the age of 13 years (with the exception of certain light agricultural or horticultural duties for a parent or guardian).
- You may only do light work and there are certain jobs which you are not allowed to do (see application form).
- There are different working hours allowed if you are under 15 or over 15.
- You must have certain rest periods.
- Your employer has to ensure that your health and safety is not at risk.
- For Year 11 pupils there is now only one school leaving date which is the last Friday in June each year. This is known as the Mandatory School Leaving Age (MSLA) in the U.K.

- Up to MSLA you can only be employed in Croydon if you have been issued with an Employment Permit from Croydon Council.
- This permit can be refused or taken away if your job is considered to be harmful to your education, health or physical development.

APPLYING FOR AN EMPLOYMENT PERMIT

Employers in Croydon are responsible for obtaining an Employment Permit for you from Croydon Council regardless of where you live.

If you live in Croydon and want to work in another area, for example, Sutton or Bromley, your employer has to apply to that Local Authority for your Employment Permit.

Application forms for employment in Croydon are available from:

EDUCATION WELFARE SERVICE
BLOCK A
SELHURST HIGH SCHOOL
THE CRESCENT
CROYDON CR0 2HN

Tel. 020 8684 4969
Fax. 020 8683 2325

Once your employer, parent/guardian and Head of Year or Head Teacher have completed and signed the Application for Employment Permit form it will be sent to the Student Services at Taberner House. If everything is all right the department will send your Employment Permit and a copy to your employer. Your school will also receive a copy.

You must carry your Employment Permit with you at all times while you are working. Your employer will keep his/her copy for inspection purposes.

Employment Permits are specific to:

You; Your Employer; the Place of Work; Type of Work and Hours of Work you do.

If any of these details change a new permit has to be issued.

Remember... *unless you are registered you may not be covered by your employer's liability insurance.*

If any of your friends have a part-time job or are considering getting one, please pass this leaflet to them. **It pays to know your rights.**

Please note: *There are specific regulations with regard to Children in Performances (theatres, T.V., films etc.). For more information, please telephone 020 8686 4433 ext. 5454.*

Croydon County Council, based on the leaflet dated November 1999

Flood alert

Many areas of England and Wales are recognised as flood risk areas. This means that approximately 5 million people, in about two million homes, are known to be affected. It is essential that all possible measures are taken to protect these people and to warn them about the risks they face. The Environment Agency plays a leading role in tackling this work.

The Environment Agency sets out to reduce the likelihood of flooding from the rivers and sea, as well as warning people about the risks they face. In order to communicate with the public, the Environment Agency publishes numerous leaflets, as well as providing up-to-date information on a number of easy-to-use Internet web pages. Access to these is gained at www.environment-agency.gov.uk/subjects/flood. The information provided is comprehensive:

- **Living on the edge**

This is a guide for owners of riverside properties, setting out their rights and responsibilities, as well as the powers and duties of the Environment Agency, Local Authorities and the Government.

- **Floodline Information**

This summarises ways to prepare for floods, and suggests strategies for coping with the consequent clear up operations.

- **Current Flood Warnings in Force**

This data is updated every 15 minutes and is available 24 hours of the day. There is access to information about all flood warnings issued in England and Wales. The country is split into eight regions, and the website allows users to search for their local area, thereby checking current local warning status.

- **Flood Management**

This explains the work of the Agency in managing and defending against floods. However, recent years have witnessed a shift away from this traditional focus on defending against flood, to a pro-active management of flood risk.

Flooding of a person's property is often a traumatic event. Nevertheless, the Environment Agency does all it can to supply information to support people. The onus is then on the individual to stay informed.

Current flood situation

National Summary for England and Wales
Page last updated: 15:45 on 18-Jan-04

	Flood Watch	Flood Warning	Severe Flood Warning	All Clear
Anglian	6	1	0	0
Midlands	0	2	0	2
Northeast	0	0	0	0
Northwest	0	0	0	0
Southern	0	0	0	0
Southwest	3	0	0	1
Thames	0	0	0	0
Wales	0	0	0	5

National Summary for England and Wales
Page last updated: 15:45 on 18-Jan-04

6 areas matched the search criteria.

You searched on the town: Welney

Click on the names of areas in the list below for further information.

Welney Causeway on the Ouse Washes		
Status:	**Flood Warning**	
Received at:	05:39 on 18-Jan-2004	
Hundred Foot River Flood Defences		
Status:	**No Warning in Force**	
Received at:	15:55 on 26-Nov-2001	
Old Bedford Counter Drain Flood Defence		
Status:	**No Warning in Force**	
Received at:	15:55 on 26-Nov-2001	
Old Pophams Eau		
Status:	**No Warning in Force**	
Received at:	12:59 on 18-Oct-2002	
River Delph Flood Defences		
Status:	**No Warning in Force**	
Received at:	15:55 on 26-Nov-2001	
Tidal Nene including Sutton Bridge and Wisbech		
Status:	**No Warning in Force**	
Received at:	15:55 on 26-Nov-2001	*Environment Agency*

Which is the pass for you?

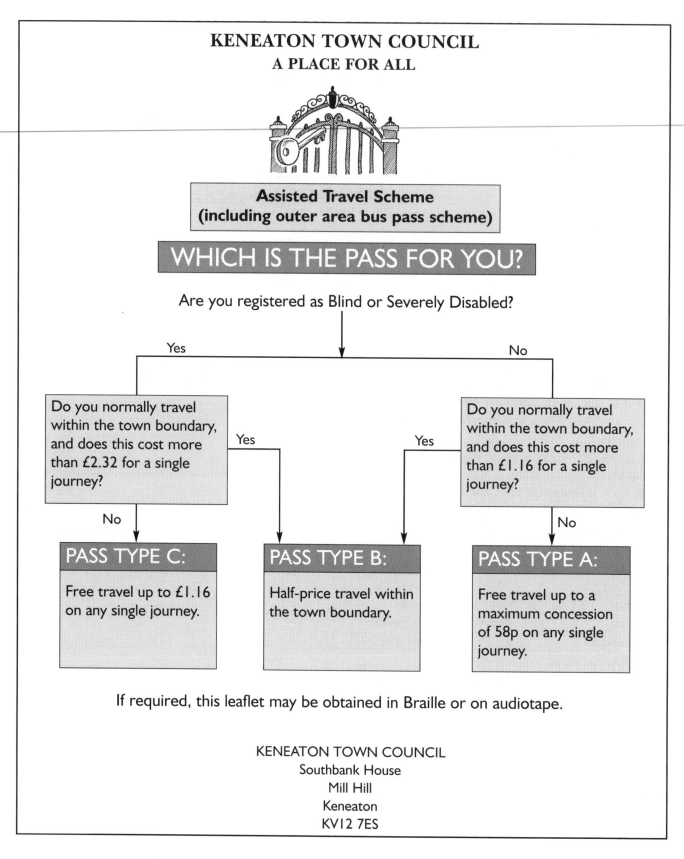

KENEATON TOWN COUNCIL
A PLACE FOR ALL

Assisted Travel Scheme
(including outer area bus pass scheme)

WHICH IS THE PASS FOR YOU?

Are you registered as Blind or Severely Disabled?

Yes

No

Do you normally travel within the town boundary, and does this cost more than £2.32 for a single journey?

Yes

Do you normally travel within the town boundary, and does this cost more than £1.16 for a single journey?

Yes

No

No

PASS TYPE C:

Free travel up to £1.16 on any single journey.

PASS TYPE B:

Half-price travel within the town boundary.

PASS TYPE A:

Free travel up to a maximum concession of 58p on any single journey.

If required, this leaflet may be obtained in Braille or on audiotape.

KENEATON TOWN COUNCIL
Southbank House
Mill Hill
Keneaton
KV12 7ES

Classworks Non-fiction Texts Year 6 © Eileen Jones, Nelson Thornes Ltd 2004

Victoria

Victoria
(1819–1901)

Victoria was the queen of Britain when it was the most powerful nation in the world. The British governed lands all around the world, giving it an empire "upon which the sun never set".

Victoria became queen when she was 18 years old. In 1840, she married her cousin, Albert, with whom she was very much in love, and with whom she had nine children. Victoria relied on Albert for help and advice. At that time Britain was changing fast, and Albert was enthusiastic about all the new technology and trade. Cotton mills and steel mills were built, and towns quickly grew into cities. Britain was the first country to manufacture vast quantities of goods cheaply. Raw materials were brought in from the countries of the empire, and Britain became rich and powerful. With Albert's encouragement, a Great Exhibition was set up in Hyde Park, London, in 1851. A huge glass pavilion was built, called the Crystal Palace, and millions of people came to see the machines and new inventions. The most important visitor was Victoria herself.

Ten years after the Great Exhibition, Albert died. Victoria was devastated and lived in seclusion for several years. Her popularity declined, but by the end of her life, she had regained it. When Victoria died, the whole empire mourned the passing of a great era.

Michael Pollard

Text 40

The worst day of my life

It was January last year. We set off for London straight after lunch. Dad was already there, as he had some work to do in London, but he had promised to take two days off, so we could all be together. Mum was feeling much better after all her hospital treatment, and I had managed to get special permission to have time off school. Life was perfect!

It was all my fault. I did the packing, as I didn't want Mum getting overtired. Of course, I had half-heard the weather forecaster's words – "severe weather warning" and "no unnecessary journeys" – but I was not an alarmist. I was also not a realist. A sensible person would have listened properly, checked an Internet report, read the newspaper, but I bothered with none of these things. I bustled around, getting our lunch and making sure that Mum was not disturbed by unnecessary, worrying reports; all she had to do was drive us to London. Dad would be waiting at the hotel.

"It's quite cold," said Mum, shivering as we emerged from the front door.

"We'll be fine in the car," I said.

For the first half-hour, everything *was* fine. Then the traffic began to slow down and the weather began to worsen. A dull day developed into a hazy light, and then the first snowflakes began to fall. It was a mere distraction at first; then it took on a more sombre note. Flakes fell faster; conditions became more difficult; Mum struggled to cope with visibility; traffic grew denser; and I began to worry.

We pulled in at the next service station, so that Mum could have a break. Her eyes were hurting and she looked tired. Anyway, I reasoned, it was only early yet, just 4.30 p.m., and there was no reason to rush. Once I had got our coffees, I gave Dad a call.

"We're just having a short break," I said. "We'll probably be with you at about 6 o'clock."

When I said where we were, he sounded anxious.

"Get your Mum on the road, Ikram. The M11 is no place to be this evening. I've heard bad reports about it. Don't get Mum into a panic, but get her going."

He was right to worry. Almost immediately, we found ourselves in traffic that was barely moving. An hour later, we had only travelled 2 miles further along the motorway. By now, it was dark, snow was falling thickly, we were stationary and Mum looked exhausted. Why hadn't I thought to bring biscuits or a drink with us? Surely she needed a heavier coat? Why had I been so desperate to have a trip to London?

I chatted to Mum, scared that she would succumb to sleep. Then I put on the radio. Was it a lifeline or a millstone? It seemed to be every other minute that programmes were interrupted by traffic reports, weather warnings and frightening news: every one of them told of desperate conditions on our motorway.

When Dad rang at eight o'clock, ten o'clock and eleven o'clock, he could only try to reassure us that we were bound to get moving soon. I found it difficult to be as optimistic. I could not voice my greatest worry: Mum's medication could need topping up. I sent Dad a text message admitting the truth: Mum's next tablets were due at midnight. She looked as if she would not be able to manage without them…

Classworks Non-fiction Texts Year 6 © Eileen Jones, Nelson Thornes Ltd 2004

Special! Special! Special!

ATL SPECIAL! SPECIAL! SPECIAL! SPECIAL! ATL
Now ANY phone, TV or computer user can...

- **WATCH** away
- **CHAT** away
- **SURF** away

We have some fantastic news for you!
This month, you can have unlimited phone calls... + digital TV... + unmetered Internet time – all in the same cheap deal from **ATL**.

WATCHING

- **50 Digital TV channels** (maximum)
- **PRIORITY upgrade offer** (according to status)
- **ACCESS to additional 80 channels** (if available)

CHATTING

- **FREE installation and connection** – no immediate payment
- **UNMETERED calls** for the first year
- **UNLIMITED units** at certain times

SURFING

- **UNMETERED Internet access** – off-peak hours
- **LIMITLESS dial-up connections in ATL network**
- **INCLUSIVE support package** (according to area)

ALL this in one cut-rate package from ATL
For just 39p a day – it's yours!

One price gives it all
One call does it all: 0800 366 4320

ATL Activating The Line

Call now – FREE!

Classworks Non-fiction Texts Year 6 © Eileen Jones, Nelson Thornes Ltd 2004

Make your lessons interactive

What you need
- An interactive whiteboard
- An electronic pen
- A computer
- Computer programs linked to the National Curriculum

How to prepare
- First think about where to position the interactive whiteboard.
- Be careful to make it visible to all pupils.
- Bear in mind that the children must be able to reach it.
- Remember that programs may have toolbars at the top of the screen: the children need to be able to reach these.
- After the board is in place, read the manufacturer's operating instructions.
- Practise using the whiteboard before teaching with it.

What to do during lessons
1. Begin to incorporate computer work into any subject – not just ICT.
2. Always have the selected program ready loaded on your laptop or PC before a lesson.
3. Treat the screen as a teaching assistant.
4. Activate it at the appropriate moment in your teaching.
5. View the program on your laptop screen while the children view it on the whiteboard.
6. **EITHER:**
   a. make changes, when necessary, to data and images on your computer screen;
   b. then watch the same changes appear on the large whiteboard.
   OR:
   a. use a finger, or the electronic pen supplied, to control the movement of objects, by touching them on the interactive whiteboard;
   b. then see the same changes matched on the small screen of the computer.
7. Make sure that the children recognise the link between the computer screen and the whiteboard.
8. Afterwards move smoothly to a different part of the program at a later point during your lesson.

Points to watch out for
- Keep the whole class involved.
- Consider letting children control the computer.
- Make sure that everyone has a chance to become confident with using the electronic pen.
- Try using the board for a group activity.
- Remember that the board should benefit learning – if it does not, ask for specialist training.
- Make regular evaluations of the contribution of your new "teaching assistant".
- Let the children enjoy the board – but make sure they keep learning!

Classworks Non-fiction Texts Year 6 © Eileen Jones, Nelson Thornes Ltd 2004

Text 43

Changes in materials

The state of materials can be changed. Such changes may be caused by actions made on the materials.

Irreversible changes

An **irreversible change** is permanent. In such a change, a material is given a completely different form. The process cannot be reversed; therefore, the new material cannot be changed back into its original state. In irreversible changes, heat is often used as the agent. Cooking contains many examples of such changes.

1. An egg is broken into a frying pan: the "white" of the egg has a clear, liquid consistency.
2. Heat is applied to the egg.
3. The "white" is changed to an opaque material.
4. The egg is removed to a cold environment.
5. The new, changed state is retained.

Similarly, when a cake is baked, irreversible changes are made: materials in their original state are replaced by the form of the final cake. The changes are made by the application of high temperatures; even if the opposite, low temperatures are applied later, as in a freezer, the original materials cannot be regained.

A similarly irreversible change is seen when coal is burned in a fire: the coal's original material is changed to ash because of the process of burning. The coal's original state cannot be recovered.

Reversible changes

Reversible changes are changes that can be temporary. If a reversible change is made to a material, that material can be restored to its original state afterwards. Such changes are caused usually by heat or cold, during the processes of melting and freezing.

For example, after the solid material of chocolate has heat applied to it, the chocolate is changed from a solid to a liquid state. However, if that liquid is then exposed to very cold temperatures, such as in a freezer, it is returned quickly to its previous solid state.

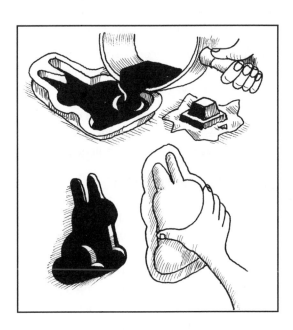

Ice cubes are also produced in a reversible change:

1. Liquid material, water, is converted into ice.
2. Because the ice is acted upon by its surrounding low temperature, it is retained in a solid state.
3. Once removed to warmer temperatures, the ice is turned back into liquid.

A similar process is seen with candle wax. Liquid melted wax can be observed dripping from a lighted candle. If the candle is extinguished, then the source of heat is removed. Consequently, the melted wax is returned to a solid form.

Text 44

How does light travel?

Most of the light on our planet comes from the Sun, but light also comes from other things including light bulbs, candles, televisions and even some kinds of animals. It travels incredibly quickly – about 300,000km (186,000 miles) per second, which is faster than anything else in the Universe.

LIGHT RAYS

Light travels in straight lines called rays. You can see this when you look at sunlight pouring in through a window or at the beam of a torch.

When light rays hit an object straight on, they are bounced back, or reflected, in the direction they came from. If the rays hit an object at an angle, they are reflected at the same angle. When light rays hit a smooth, shiny surface, such as a mirror, they are all reflected in the same direction, but if they hit a rough surface, they are reflected in many directions.

BRIGHTNESS

Any object that gives off light is described as luminous. The level of brightness of the light is called its intensity.

The further you are from a source of light, the less intense the light is. This is because light rays spread out as they travel away from their source.

Most objects aren't luminous. We can only see them because they are reflecting light from something that is luminous, such as the sun or a light bulb.

SHINING THROUGH

Some things allow light to shine through them and others don't. Substances that allow lots of light to shine through them, such as clear glass, are described as transparent. Those that only allow a little light through, such as frosted glass, are said to be translucent. Substances that won't allow any light to shine through them are described as opaque. Most substances are opaque. Light rays bounce off them instead of travelling through them. When light shines on an opaque object, a shadow forms on the other side of the object.

Usborne Publishing

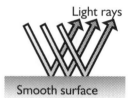
Light rays

Smooth surface

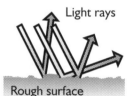
Light rays

Rough surface

These two diagrams show how light rays are reflected off smooth and rough surfaces.

Here you can see light rays shining through gaps in the trees. This shows that light travels in straight lines.

BENDING LIGHT

If you look at a straw in a glass of water, the straw looks bent. This is because light rays travel at different speeds through different materials. They travel faster through air than through water, but faster through water than through glass. The change in speed makes the light rays bend, or refract.

Text 45

How can rivers change?

A river changes as it flows downhill along its path, or course. The beginning of a river is called its source. Many rivers begin in mountain areas, where rain and melting ice run into steep, clear streams. These streams cut narrow, deep valleys and join together as they flow downhill. Smaller streams and rivers that flow into a bigger river are called tributaries.

Away from the mountains, the water flows in broader channels and larger valleys. As the land levels out, the river starts to form large bends, or meanders. Finally, the river widens out into a broad estuary, or splits to form a network of channels called a delta, before flowing into the sea or a lake. The part of the river where it meets the sea is called the river mouth.

RIVERS AT WORK

As a river flows, the water sweeps along any rocks in its way. The rocks slide and bounce along, chipping away at the riverbed and making it deeper and wider. They also grind against each other, which wears them down and breaks them into smaller pieces.

As a river flows downstream, the riverbed becomes smoother, so the water flows slightly faster. It starts to drop or deposit, sand, silt and then mud. This is why the lower sections of a river have muddy riverbeds. Near the sea, the sediment may build up to form whole islands. This is when the river splits up to form a delta.

These rocks have been smoothed and rounded by the action of the water in the river.

Usborne Publishing

Classworks Non-fiction Texts Year 6 © Eileen Jones, Nelson Thornes Ltd 2004

How can rivers change? (continued)

CHANGING COURSE

Rivers flow faster around the outside of a bend, or meander, than on the inside. The outside edge is gradually eroded while the river deposits sediment on the inside edge. This means that the meander grows longer and narrower over time.

Eventually, the two sides of the meander meet each other and the river cuts through to form a new, straighter course. The entrance to the meander gradually fills up with sediment, and the loop is cut off leaving a lake called an oxbow lake or a billabong.

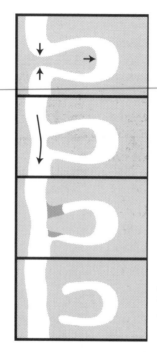

A river erodes the outside of a bend and deposits sediment on the inside making a loop.

The loop grows longer and narrower until the river finally breaks through.

The river flows past the ends of the loop and they slowly become silted up.

Eventually, the loop gets cut off completely and forms an oxbow lake.

WATERFALLS

Waterfalls begin when a river flows from an area of hard rock onto soft rock. The river wears away the soft rock more quickly and creates a ledge. Water falling over the ledge erodes a hollow at the bottom called a plunge pool. The bigger the ledge, the greater the force of the water crashing down. The action of the water and pebbles churning in the plunge pool can undercut the hard rock, creating an overhanging ledge. Chunks of the overhanging rock break off and very gradually, over hundreds of years, the waterfall moves backwards, cutting a deep valley called a gorge.

This diagram shows how a waterfall is formed.

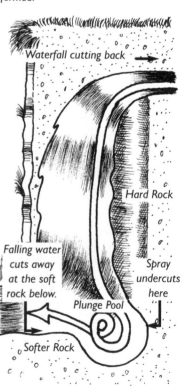

Waterfall cutting back →

Hard Rock

Falling water cuts away at the soft rock below.

Spray undercuts here

Plunge Pool

Softer Rock

Usborne Publishing

Text 47

House of Russell

Christmas Lines

Christmas lines are not moving. House of Russell has its largest ever range of Christmas goods. No expense has been spared and all areas of merchandise have been covered. Nevertheless, things are not going well for us.

This report sets out areas in which House of Russell is experiencing its greatest difficulties and suggests strategies to be adopted.

Ladies' clothing

The weather is unseasonably mild, with these temperatures predicted to last over the coming month. Our coat sales are suffering. A real push is needed in every store, with the following incentives offered to customers:

- £25 discount made on every coat costing £90 or more;
- £50 House of Russell voucher, to be spent in January, given away with every coat costing £150 or more;
- a free co-ordinating accessory item included in the purchase of every coat.

One point needs to be kept in mind: if a coat is not sold by Christmas, it is likely still to be with us until next year. We need the profit **NOW**.

Seasonal stationery

Most branches are suffering because of the price war between *Millstones* and *All Cards*. With Christmas stationery, experience proves that customers buy wrapping paper and assorted wrappings when they buy cards. Marketing our cards must be an urgent priority.

Therefore, we have no choice but to cut prices – and we need to do it **NOW**. All our card prices are reduced by a third from today. All branches need to run an aggressive advertising campaign, so that customers know what is happening.

Jewellery

Jewellery space is limited in most branches and this area of merchandising is now running at a loss. Numerous sales drives and promotional offers have yielded poor results and sale figures remain disappointing. The company takes the view that House of Russell should pull out of this market.

Present stock may be sold off as branches see fit, with a special drive in the last two weeks before Christmas. Effective use of stock could be made in the form of free gifts, creating incentives in the sale of more profitable lines, such as perfume and ladies' leather goods.

Children's toys

Sales figures here are not unreasonable, but they could be better. The new action doll lines are our top sellers in every store. More deliveries are imminent, and no branch should allow themselves to run out. The aim must be to make all our toy departments irresistible: pull the children in and the parents have no choice but to buy.

Electrical goods

We are not competitive. *Magnus* and *Ajax* are undercutting House of Russell in most lines. Every store must have in place a tracking system of local prices. Daily checks need to be made, and, if necessary, prices cut. We have to be the **CHEAPEST**.

All branches have a large stock of computers and games machines. Research tells us that customers want them: all we have to do is to make sure they are buying from us.

Classworks Non-fiction Texts Year 6 © Eileen Jones, Nelson Thornes Ltd 2004

Text 48

Modern environmental problems

Environmental problems are one of the key issues facing the world at the present time. The growth of industry and economic activity since the Second World War has caused serious pollution on a global scale and is putting an increasing strain on natural resources. At the same time, there has been a massive increase in population. Human numbers have more than trebled since the start of the twentieth century and are likely to go on rising. Ultimately, there is a limit to the demands that can be put on the Earth which is a finite system.

A number of other factors have compounded the problem. One of them is inequality. About one-fifth of the world's population currently consume about four-fifths of the world's wealth. This leaves the vast majority impoverished. The contrast between the developed countries of the 'North' and developing countries of the 'South' was highlighted by the Brandt Report in 1980. Ultimately, the environmental crisis, which is the product of human activity, will only be solved when there is a much greater measure of social justice.

In recent years, there have been some serious efforts to address the problem. The Earth Summit that was held in Rio de Janeiro in 1992 was a major landmark in international cooperation and was attended by representatives from many of the world's nations. One of the outcomes was a blueprint for the planet which has come to be known as Agenda 21. Another was the notion of sustainable development.

Schools throughout Britain have enthusiastically adopted these ideas. Schemes to recycle waste and reduce consumption are widespread. Specific projects such as Eco-schools (run by the Tidy Britain Group) have also proved popular. Activities of this kind are central components in a curriculum focused on citizenship and environmental awareness.

Research findings

Even before they come to school, children acquire ideas about the environment. However, many of these notions are incomplete or confused. For example, when nursery children were asked about creatures which live in polar lands, Palmer (1998) found about a third gave completely inappropriate answers. Similarly, junior school children appear to have very muddled ideas about the greenhouse effect. In a survey of 563 children, Qualter (1995) found that 85 per cent thought that protecting rare species would help to alleviate the problem. A similar number believed that reducing nuclear bombs would be the solution. These findings are a timely reminder that, although children today have access to a lot of information about the world around them, they need help in making sense of it.

Stephen Scoffham, Colin Bridge, Terry Jewson

Text 49

Glossary

potential energy Energy that is stored, ready to be used.

precipitation Rain, snow, hail or any other water falling from the sky.

Prime Meridian Line An imaginary line that runs from north to south through Greenwich, England, at zero degrees of longitude.

program A set of instructions that enables a computer to carry out certain tasks.

proton A positively charged particle in the *nucleus* of an *atom*.

refraction The change in direction of light rays as they enter a different medium.

reptile Any of a class of scaly, cold-blooded animals that lay eggs.

rift valley A valley formed when land collapses between two *faults* in the Earth's *crust*.

satellite An object that orbits a *planet* or *star*. Some, such as the Moon, are natural, but many are built to do particular jobs, such as monitoring the weather.

scale The size of a map in relation to the area it represents. If a map's scale is 1:100, 1cm on the map represents 100cm of the area shown.

sedimentary rock Rock made up of particles of sand, mud and other debris that have settled on the seabed and been squashed down.

software The *programs* used by a computer.

Solar System The *Sun* and the *planets* and other objects that orbit it.

solar wind A constant stream of invisible particles blown out into space from the *Sun*.

sonar A method of bouncing sounds off objects and measuring the results. Sonar is used to map the seabed.

species A type of animal or plant.

stamen The male reproductive organ of a plant, consisting of a stalk with an *anther* at the end.

star A huge ball of gas in space that gives out heat and light. The *Sun* is a star.

static electricity Electrical charge held by a material.

stigma The sticky part of a *carpel* that catches *pollen*.

stratosphere A layer in the middle of the *atmosphere*. It contains the ozone layer.

stratus A type of cloud that forms low in the sky in flat, grey layers.

streamlined Designed to allow a gas or a liquid to flow smoothly around something.

style The part of a *carpel* that connects the *stigma* to the *ovary*.

Sun The *star* that lies in the middle of our *Solar System*.

temperate A *climate* that is characterised by mild temperatures.

tendon A tough band of tissue that attaches a muscle to a bone.

thermosphere A layer in the *atmosphere* between the *mesophere* and the *exosphere*, where the temperature can reach up to 1500°C (2732°F).

thrust The *force* that moves some vehicles forwards.

time zone A region where the same standard time is used.

translucent Allowing some light to pass through.

transparent Allowing light to pass through.

trench A long, deep channel in the ocean floor.

tributary A river that flows into a bigger river.

trophic level A level of a *food chain*

troposphere The lowest layer of the Earth's *atmosphere*.

tsunami A giant wave caused by an *earthquake*, *landslide* or volcanic activity on the seabed.

tundra A *climate* characterised by harsh winds and low winter temperatures.

Universe The collection of everything that exists in space.

vein A *blood vessel* that carries blood to the heart.

vertebrate A animal with a spine.

volcano An opening in the Earth's surface from which lava rock fragments, ash and gases are ejected.

weight A measure of strength of the pull of *gravity* on an object.

Usborne Publishing

Text 50

Different types of poetry

In this dictionary you will find different types of poetry to inspire you. Have a go at writing your own poems based on the types below.

Haiku (see pages 33, 45)
These short poems come from Japan. They are usually three lines long and have a pattern of 5/7/5 syllables. You can also use your own syllable pattern.

Cinquain (see pages 19, 59)
These are like haiku. They have five lines and use a pattern of 2/4/6/8/2 syllables. You can also invent your own syllable pattern.

Limericks (see page 68)
These are often funny and usually have three long lines and two short ones. The rhyming pattern is aa/bb/a.

Riddles (see page 28)
These are fun to write. Try to give clues without giving the subject away.

Acrostics (see page 91)
These poems spell out a word in letters hidden somewhere within the lines. You read acrostics downwards.

Calligrams (see pages 54–55)
These are written so that the shape of the words reflect the meaning. On page 54 the letters of the words "rolling pin" form the shape of a rolling pin.

Rhyming couplets (see page 71)
These are two lines which rhyme. You can invent other rhyming patterns, as in the poem on page 83, which uses the pattern aa/bb/a.

Word plays (see pages 41, 93)
Some poems play with words by taking them literally.

Rhyming games

Pass the rhyme
This is a quick game you can play anywhere. The first player says a word and the next has to say a rhyming word. The rhyming sound is passed on until no-one can think of another rhyming word.

Place names
This is a good game for journeys. Try finding rhymes for place names, or people's names, for example:

*I felt loud
in Stroud
picked my teeth
in Moncrieff…*

Copycat
Think of a well-known nursery rhyme or song and copy it, changing some of the words. Look at the alternative version of Humpty Dumpty on page 14.

Pie Corbett and Ruth Thomson

Classworks Non-fiction Texts Year 6 © Eileen Jones, Nelson Thornes Ltd 2004

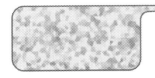

Teaching notes and ideas

Journalistic writing

1 First night review

Discuss the likely context and purpose. Talk about journalistic writing, identifying key style features (arresting headline; powerful vocabulary; facts and opinions). Is this a successful review? **T12**

Investigate real newspaper reviews (for example for the theatre, the cinema or television). Ask the children to evaluate their language, style and success. **T12**

Is there a film, play or television programme which everyone has seen? Ask the children to write a review of it for the next day's newspaper. **T16**

2 End of the rote

Investigate journalistic style in this text from a teaching magazine. Which features are important? (Names; quotes; facts and figures; accuracy; informative first sentence.) List points made, distinguishing the modern Moscow school from traditional Moscow counterparts. Compare your school with the modern Moscow school. **T15**

Explain 'balanced reporting'. Is this report balanced? Is a quote from a parent needed? Why? **T15**

Ask the children to identify connectives. Which connectives are useful in a balanced report? ('However', 'even', 'although', 'but', 'on the other hand'.) Use other texts or thesauri for support. **S4**

3 British weather hits the headlines

Discuss the likely context. (A British national daily newspaper/science section of newspaper/weather section/magazine.) Consider: presentation (headings; different sections); content (facts and figures; information likely to be of most interest). **T15**

Provide science or geography magazines and reports; focus on a relevant topic. Ask the children to review and comment critically on journalistic style. Does the writer select and present information well? Is the reporting balanced and ethical? **T12, T15**

4 It's good to talk

Analyse the style, structure and content of this piece. Stress the writer's wish to be scrupulously fair. How is this obvious? (Constant references to all sides and points of view.)

Ask the children to identify points made in favour of or against e-mail? Which argument is made more strongly? How? **T15**

Imagine that the editor needs the article to take up less space. How can this be shortened? What can be left out? Stress the need for balance. Set a limit of about 350–400 words. **T8**

5–6 The London Chronicle

Point out that Text 5 is a true story. Why did the editor use it as a lead story? (Current news; importance; interest.) Examine journalistic conventions and style. Which features are important? (Stress capital letters; bold font; columns; headlines.) **T16**

Let the children work in pairs to work on a lead story for this evening's newspaper. Compare results. **T16**

Ask the children to list information given about London and its traffic in Text 6. Use a person, event or situation in the current news to list a similar number of points. Can you write the newspaper story to fit this space. **T8**

Do sentence level work, reconstructing sentences, or altering word order. Study the 'Playground' story. Ask the children to adapt it, for younger children. **S1**

Brainstorm ideas for a class newspaper. Focus on current events, stressing accuracy and conciseness. Allow time for revision, editing and the use of ICT. **T18**

7 January 2003
What is the likely context? Can the children identify it as piece of radio journalism? How could they tell? Discuss the similarities between journalistic styles for different media. **T15**

Point out how the sections 12.30 a.m. and 2.00 a.m. are actually addressing the listener, as opposed to other sections where reporting is taking place. **T15**

Brainstorm ideas for a radio report (a recent local or school event). Ask the children to prepare the report. **T16**

Speaking and listening
Listen to one another's radio reports.

Share some of the writing resulting from Text 6. Encourage the children to offer constructive comments.

Discuss what the children have learned about journalistic writing.

Autobiography and biography

8 Who is Alan Gibbons?
Introduce the words 'autobiography' and 'biography'. What is the difference? Identify key features in this piece of biographical writing (third person; important incidents in the subject's life; chronological order). **T11**

Talk about fact and opinion. Can the children differentiate between the two? **T11**

Use the opening as the basis for a discussion on 'Books I couldn't put down'. **T5**

9–10 Michael Morpurgo
Investigate the structure of this biography, as the writer, Joanna Carey, moves between first and third person. How did she find out details of time, names and places? Is she relating facts or expressing opinions? **T14**

Use the term CV. Ask the children to compile personal CVs. **T14**

Hold a class discussion on literature by Michael Morpurgo; or discuss literature that the children enjoy. How does it affect you, the reader? **T3**, **T4**

Discuss Carey's inclusion of the questions she asks Michael Morpurgo. Is this a good way to write the biography? Why? What are the advantages and disadvantages? Why are some parts in italics? (Carey's own comments.) **T11**

Talk about the children's own experiences as writers. Is there an overlap between fact and fiction?

Use Texts 8 and 9 as models for a biographical account of another author. Write to an author, invite one in or use a website for research. These are helpful sites: *www.channel4.com/learning/microsites/B/bookbox* and *www.mystworld.com/youngwriter/authors* **T14**

11 Friends and locals

Point out that this writing is autobiographical. Which words show this? ('my', 'I' and 'we'.) Consider how the same text would be written as a biography. Is one form better than the other? **T11**

Discuss personal responses to this text. Was his childhood appealing or strange? How does it differ from the children's experiences today? When are the events set? (World War Two.) Which references date the experiences? **T3**, **T5**

Do you think that early experiences influence fiction? Consider examples. **T4**

12 The Diary of a Young Girl

Let the children do research into the background of this autobiographical writing. Compare it with Text 11. Do you respond differently to Anne's account? Stress the importance of the first person. **T3**

Hold group discussions on the two war texts, ensuring that the children all have the chance to contribute and to build on the views expressed by others. **T5**

Identify different connecting devices used in complex sentences. Use substitute links, perhaps altering the structure and sequence of the clauses. Is the meaning affected? **S5**

13 Anne Frank: A girl who wanted to be heard

Point out the past tense, chronological order, and formal tone (assisted by the passive voice). Why is formality appropriate in biographies? (A focus on facts, not personal opinions.) **T11**

Focus on the construction of complex sentences. Let the children experiment with other clause links, working with a response partner: Does this sentence make sense? Has the meaning become confused? Which link is better? **S5**

14 My life

Ask the children to identify key features (focus on the writer; first person; mention of main events in the writer's life; chronological order; past tense). Stress that an autobiography can reflect the writer's personality. What impressions do you get of Victoria? Distinguish between implicit and explicit points. Help the children to identify examples. (Explicit: Victoria Falls is named after me; Implicit: I want to be remembered.) **T11**

Select key figures from your current history topic. Ask the children to research their lives, and to write autobiographies in appropriate voices. **T14**

15 Launched on the Clyde

How do you react to this text? Would it be as effective in the third person? Compare views. **T3**

Compare it with Text 14. Does the writing style express the author's personality? Read an extract from the autobiography of another sportsperson.

Investigate examples of complex sentences, exploring the effect on meaning of the sequence and structure of clauses. **S5**

16 The Football Hall of Fame

Compare this with the previous text. Which do you find more interesting? Which is more revealing about the subject? Debate the advantages and disadvantages of first and third person writing.

Ask the children to identify clause links. Are the writer's selections appropriate? Let the children experiment with new clause links. **S5**

Ask the children to write the top section as continuous prose, creating complex sentences, and paying attention to their selection of connecting devices. Listen to and evaluate one another's choices.

Speaking and listening

Hold a class discussion on this type of writing. Do the children enjoy reading about the lives of other people? Does it bring the past to life?

Share some of the autobiographies based on Text 14.

Reports

17 A guide to the River Severn

What type of text is this? (Non-chronological report.) Ask the children to identify important features: random order; introduction to orientate the reader; descriptive language; present tense verbs; impersonal style. **T13**

Revise the terms 'active' and 'passive'. Explain that the use of passive verbs can make the information more general and impersonal. Collaborate in identifying examples. Give practice in transforming sentences from active to passive, and vice versa. Does the word order need to change? Are there subtle changes in meaning? **S2, S3**

18 The Thames

Ask the children to identify the features found in Text 17. Are there additional ones? (Headings.) Point out that headings commonly feature in non-chronological reports. **T13**

Link report writing to your geography work. Ask the children to plan a report on a relevant river or a mountain environment. **T17**

19 Flooding

This report is in the form of an urgent radio broadcast; it describes the way things are. Ask the children to identify report features. **T13**

Do the children know anything of this event? Can they find out more? (Internet; parents.) Ask them to write reports sent in from low-lying villages in the area. **T17**

Can you link this to your geography work? Ask the children to plan a report on changes now obvious in a river or mountain region. **T17**

20 Report on flood damage to local area

Ask the children to identify examples of key features. Emphasise the introduction, which orientates the reader. Ask the children to identify examples of key features. Investigate where and when different types of language are used (for example, descriptive and impersonal language types). **T13**

Write the reports planned for Text 19. **T17**

21 Food for the Ancient Greeks

What text type is this? (Non-chronological report.) What do you notice about the verbs? (Past tense, because of the subject matter.) Identify similar features to those in Texts 17 and 18. **T13**

Provide further practice in identifying active and passive verbs. Ask the children to transform some sentences from active to passive, or vice versa. **S2**

22 The modern use of the ideas of Ancient Greece

Provide the children with a list of features to identify. Ask for two or three examples of each. **T13**

Provide etymological dictionaries. Ask the children to compile word lists for Greek prefixes (philo-; astro-; sym-; mono-; tri-). Stress the need to understand meanings of prefixes and words. Add some of the words to the children's spelling logs and let them devise strategies for learning to spell them. **W3**

Speaking and listening

Hold an oral review of the features of non-chronological reports.

Put the children in twos to share their own reports. Encourage response partners to offer useful questions and comments, such as 'I think you need more impersonal terms', 'Why is there no introduction to orientate the reader?', 'I think you are using passive verbs well'.

Make sure that the children are using the correct terminology of report writing in their discussions.

TERM 2

Argument

23 Dear Mr Whallen

Focus on content. What is Matthew's request? How does he argue his case? Which points are persuasive?

Refer to the sentence beginning 'As for the people who live nearby'. Discuss why Matthew mentions these people. Is he wise to do so? Point out that he is pre-empting a possible objection: the people nearby would not like the ramp. Is the letter likely to be successful? **T15**

Ask the children to add a further point(s) to the letter. **T18**

24 Dear Ms Clarke

Analyse the structure. Are effective techniques employed? (Persuasive, emotive expression of points; answers possible objections, with mention of an alternative place to play; supporting evidence, with mention of increase in medication; appeal to audience's known view on noise pollution.) **T15**

Ask the children to write a new letter, putting forward a well-linked argument. **T18**

25 Proposed building of a skateboarding ramp in Talisman Square (For)

Discuss style. Do the children recognise this speech as an argument? How many sides are represented? Ask them to investigate the construction of the argument: points made; how they are linked; supporting evidence; how potential objections (such as cost) are pre-empted and answered; how audience sympathy is gained. Compare findings. **T15**

26 Proposed building of a skateboarding ramp in Talisman Square (Against)

Analyse the argument's construction. Make comparisons with the last text. Which is more effective? Why? **T15**

Use the two texts for sentence level work, identifying examples of conditionals. Model write further examples of the use of conditionals. **S5**

27 The Chairman's Report

Which side of the argument is this on? What makes the Chair's report balanced? (Fair summary of the competing views; analysis of the strengths and weaknesses of different positions.)

When does the text stop being a balanced report? (The last part, where the Chairman expresses a personal opinion: the venture should go ahead.) **T16**

Examine further the formation and use of conditional sentences. Work with the children, identifying examples. Use some as models for the children's own sentences; or play the 'If' game. ('Grammar for Writing' Unit 51.) **S5**

28 Proposition for debate (For)

Explain what a debate is. Stress the formality of much of the language. What points are made in support of a four term year? Ask the children to identify connectives linking the points in the argument. **T15**

Investigate the structure of the conditional sentences. Use some of them as models for further oral practice, in order to give confidence with verb tense. **S5**

29 Proposition for debate (Against)

Compare this with the previous text. Identify points of similarity. Point out how one fact (children's concern about moving from Key Stage 2 to 3) can be used to support either opinion.

Ask the children to evaluate both texts. Do the arguments have particular strengths and weaknesses? Which points do you find most persuasive? **T15**

30 The Chair's summing up of the debate

Which side of the argument is this text on? Point out that the Chair's summing up begins with an abbreviated version of the preceding two texts. What is the final section? (It highlights some strengths and weaknesses in the arguments.) Stress that the Chair presents a balanced report, not her own views. **T16**

Brainstorm ideas for a class debate. Look for a topic that is both relevant and controversial. Ask the children to prepare structured arguments. **T18**

After holding the debate, in a Speaking and Listening session ask the children to write a summing-up in the form of a balanced report. **T19**

Speaking and listening

Hold the class debate, using the correct formal language.

Encourage the children to listen to and acknowledge other points of view.

Formal writing

31 Particular aspects of negligence: children

Legal documents contain very formal language. Why is this necessary? (Need for unambiguous definitions and statements.)

Do the children know the term 'footnotes'? Explain that they are printed at the bottom of a page, and contain information which is additional to that contained in the main body of the text. **T17**

Discuss the fact that in order to avoid any ambiguity, 'legalese' can prove very difficult for ordinary people to understand. Ask the children to try to explain the text more simply. **T20**

Formal writing is likely to involve the use of the passive voice. Revise the terms 'active' and 'passive', and make clear the distinction:

You <u>see</u> an example – active;

An example is <u>seen</u> – passive.

Investigate the text, identifying examples of active and passive verbs. Experiment with changing one to the other. What impact can a change have on meaning? **S1**

32 Rules of golf

Why is there so much detail? Why are explanations so precise? (To avoid misinterpretation.) Point out how formal the language is, although the subject matter is only a game.

Consider presentation and key features. Why are some words italicised? (These words, and their definitions, are listed in an earlier section of the book.)

Do you have written rules for sports played at your school? Compare them. Do any words and expressions prove to be typical? **S2**

33 Ill-health retirement

Discuss the importance of this information to people. Is it easy to understand? Investigate: (i) **presentation**: headings; sections (ii) **content and style**: formal, precise language; repetition of words and terms (pensionable employment); detail; the references to other sources of information; specific terms and names. **T17**

Can the children understand the document? Point out that its language is not aimed at their age group. Work together, simplifying a section.

34–35 Hours of work

Who is the intended reader of this pamphlet? How do you know? (References directed to the child.) Does this affect the layout and language of the text? (Compare with Text 33.)

Discuss the importance of such information and the problems caused by not understanding it. What should the text be like? (Clear; correct facts; no room for misunderstanding; information on how to proceed further.) Investigate (i) presentation, and (ii) content and style. **T17**

Is the text successful – can the children understand it? Test this by putting the children into small groups or pairs, and set questions on the pamphlet. Compare answers. **T20**

Set the task of writing an 'official' document linked to your school (for example, the right to use parts of school or school property). Allow plenty of time for planning, drafting, editing and final production of the text.

36 Flood Alert

Search the text for examples of active and passive verbs. Experiment with the transformation from active to passive and vice versa. Point out how sentences can be re-ordered. **S1**

37 Current flood situation

Explain that this is information taken from the Internet website of the Environment Agency. Discuss the importance and need for comprehension. Is it more manageable than Text 33? What makes its layout user-friendly? Is visual representation easier to understand than formal, official language? **T17**

The person using the website lives in Welney. Write the report that he will now post on his local information board.

38 Which is the pass for you?

Discuss the style and format. Point out that this is set out as a simple questionnaire. Subsequent information depends on the answer given by the reader, so the language must be very specific. Is the information easy to access? **T17**

Investigate the construction and language of the final section. Stress the impersonal voice of the document. Are there passive verbs? **S1**, **S2**

Refer back to the writing done for Text 35. Ask the children to write a questionnaire to help children to acquire the school pass suited to their age and needs. Stress the need to follow appropriate language conventions. **S2**

Speaking and listening

Discuss what the class has learned about the characteristic features of formal, standard English.

Listen to some of the children's own writing.

Encourage discussion of the texts. Does it read well? Is the language impersonal enough?

TERM 3

Reading and writing non–fiction

39 Victoria

Identify this as a recount. Revise key language conventions and grammatical features: written in the third person; past tense; introductory paragraph to orientate reader; time connectives; chronological sequence; closing statement. **S1**

Compare this with Text 13. Point out that biographies and autobiographies are likely to be written as recounts. What other contexts are likely for recounts? (History books; newspaper reports; anecdotes; accounts of personal experiences.) **T19**

40 The worst day of my life

How is this similar to Text 39? What is the big difference between the two recounts? This one is written in the first person, instead of the third person; it describes personal feelings and experiences. Can the children think of examples in their own writing when they have done this? **T19**

Identify some of the language conventions and grammatical features observed in Text 39. Why is there no closing statement? (This is part of the recount.) **S1**

Ask the children to write a recount of their observations and experiences during the school adventure week or a recent field trip. Decide on the audience, and stress the need to make the style appropriate. **T22**

41 Special! Special! Special!

What text type is this? (Persuasive.) Revise key features (attracting the reader's attention; persuasive words; deliberate ambiguity.)

Point out 'maximum' and 'according to area'. Ask the children to identify other examples of deliberate ambiguity. Why has the writer used them? **T19**

Stress the need to identify a target audience and to use words that will appeal to those people. Who is the target audience for this leaflet? Which words are likely to be effective? How important is presentation? Does this leaflet work? **T19**, **S1**

42 Make your lessons interactive

What text type is this? (Instructional.) When or where is it likely to be used? (A teaching manual; a training session.) **T19**

Revise key language conventions and grammatical features. What do you notice about the verbs? (Present tense; imperatives.) What is an imperative verb's usual position in the sentence? (At the beginning.) Point out: strict adherence to chronological steps; supporting time words ('then'; 'now'); clear layout; organisational devices. **S1**

Provide test practice in writing instructions, specifying topic and audience. Let the children test their writing on one another. **T22**

Explanations

43 Changes in materials

Discuss likely contexts for explanations (science textbooks or experiments; encyclopaedia; machine manuals). Revise key language and grammatical features. Stress the formality of the language and sentence construction; clarity; emphasis on logical order; the use of time connectives, and causal connectives. Ask the children to identify examples of causal language ('caused by'; 'turned back'; 'because'; 'consequently'). **T15**, **T19**

Model write an explanation on a process recently studied in science. **T22**

44 How does light travel?

Stress the purpose of an explanation: to explain how or why a process occurs. Point out the relevance of the title, as it establishes content. How is the reader helped to understand the explanation? Can the children identify examples of passive verbs? What effect does the passive voice have on tone and style? (More formal.) **S1**

Use a recent science investigation for further writing practice. **T22**

Speaking and listening

Focus on explanatory texts: review characteristics, and discuss why each is important.

Hold a question and answer session. How are children constructing their answers? Are they analysing questions? Are they able to formulate replies?

Impersonal writing

Explanations

45–46 How can rivers change?

Investigate style (formal and impersonal). How is it achieved? (Correct 'technical' vocabulary; sustained use of present tense; passive voice.) **T16**

Use the paragraph beginning 'As a river flows, ...' for the children to change into the passive voice. Which version is better? Why? **T20**

Focus on sentence construction and punctuation. Identify examples of complex sentences. How are clauses linked? Which clause is subordinate? What is a causal connective? Use text sentences as models for the children's own writing. **S3**

Reports

47 House of Russell

What text type is this? (A report.) Explain that a report describes the way things are. Point out the opening statement and the use of generic terms ('electrical goods'; 'accessory item'). **T16**, **S3**

Use the text for comprehension work. How quickly can the children retrieve information needed to answer your questions? **T17**

Ask the children to plan and write reports relevant to your school (current use of school clubs) or the local environment (the use made of the public library). **T20**

48 Modern environmental problems

Present this report as the result of research into modern environmental problems, and children's knowledge of them. Stress the impersonal, formal tone. How do the verbs contribute to this? (Frequent use of the passive voice.) Ask the children to identify examples. **T16**

How quickly and accurately can the children retrieve information from the report? Provide sample questions: for example, 'Where was the Earth Summit held?' Discuss how the answer is found, and the reading skills used. Let the children continue this exercise with a partner. Could the text be improved so that information could be retrieved more efficiently? (Use of headings, for example.) **T17**

Ask the children to add to this text, supplying information on another project or area of environmental concern (a wildlife issue; town planning; energy resources). Model write an opening sentence. Stress the need to maintain an impersonal style. Encourage the use of the present tense and the passive voice. **T20**

Reference texts

49 Glossary

Consider the source and type of text. (Part of the glossary in a science reference book.) How is the text arranged? Is its use straightforward? Would it be useful for this class? **T16**

Ask the children to extend the glossary, with vocabulary relevant to Year 6 curriculum topics. Stress the need for an impersonal style of writing. **T20**

50 Different types of poetry

What is the source of this text? (A literary reference book.) Ask the children to make a quick appraisal of its usefulness to them. What informs their decision?

Practise using the text efficiently: Which page might be useful for _____? Try the same exercise with reference pages in classroom textbooks, so that the children can identify whether their initial evaluations are sound. **T17**

Speaking and listening

Share views on retrieving information. Which types of sources do you prefer? Which skills do you use?

Ask the children to make oral appraisals of some non-fiction texts. Does this appear useful? What is your method of judging?